Crosscurrents / MODERN CRITIQUES

Harry T. Moore, *General Editor*

HAROLD PINTER

The Poetics of Silence

James R. Hollis

PREFACE BY
Harry T. Moore

SOUTHERN ILLINOIS UNIVERSITY PRESS
Carbondale and Edwardsville

FEFFER & SIMONS, INC.
London and Amsterdam

Copyright © 1970, by Southern Illinois University Press
All rights reserved
Printed in the United States of America
Designed by Andor Braun
ISBN 0–8093–0450–3
Library of Congress Catalog Card Number 77–86186

Contents

Preface

In giving the subtitle The Poetics of Silence to his book on
Harold Pinter, James R. Hollis shows how up to date he is,
for these days we have various studies on the language of
silence, the literature of silence, and the theater of silence.
But Mr. Hollis is doing something more than being in the
main current, for silence is one of Pinter's principles of technique; consider, for example, in his early success, The Caretaker, how many times the stage direction pause is used.

Pauses and dramatic actions taking place without the use
of words are of course no new thing in the theater. In the
tragedies of ancient Athens, tableaux were popular: the fas-
tidious dramatists placed their tragic scenes offstage, and the
bloody events were described by a messenger or some other
supernumerary; but the "managers" put the actors on a cart
they rolled in, the ekkyklema, so that the populace could see
a frozen version of the horrible events. One school of thought
believes that in Shakespeare's time pauses hardly existed; the
actors all spoke their lines "trippingly" and didn't observe
pauses; at least the plays on the Bankside went rapidly, according to the notes on timing we have. In 1924, when John
Barrymore played Hamlet in London, he received a shrewdly
witty letter from Bernard Shaw, criticizing him for his many
pauses (during which he usually sawed the air with his pro-
file—I saw this); Barrymore, Shaw complained, used only
about half of Shakespeare's text and yet his production took
up more time than full-length performances at Shakespeare's
own Globe.

But most recent actors and directors have made extensive

use of pause, pantomime, and suggestion. We still hear of the famous last exit of Sarah Bernhardt in that claptrap but once enormously popular melodrama, Madame X. Bernhardt, in going out the door, clung to one side of it with her hand, which was soon all that was seen of her, the audience aching as she withdrew one supposedly anguished finger after another until she was completely gone.

As for today's theater of silence, it has a possible ancestry in some of the productions of the Moscow Art Theater under Constantin Stanslavsky. And there are some of the French plays of the early 1920s, such as Jean-Jaques Bernard's Martine and The Springtime of Others, in which a good deal of the central meaning is not conveyed in words but by action of various kinds, pantomimed or otherwise suggested.

It is interesting to note that, before Harold Pinter took up playwriting, he was an actor, playing often in Shakespearan companies such as Sir Donald Wolfit's, in which pauses were frequently and rather heavily used to underline the meanings of speeches. Early in the present book, Mr. Hollis tells us the circumstances under which Pinter wrote his first play, The Room (1957); in his chapter on this and two of Pinter's subsequent plays, Mr. Hollis deals with rooms used as metaphors in these early dramas and then, in other chapters, as in some of the later dramas—in his course of exploration of this room metaphor (we used to say symbol, didn't we?), Mr. Hollis has some important points to make, which greatly help us to understand Pinter.

And this applies to all the plays discussed, with special treatment of the notable successes such as The Caretaker and The Homecoming. Mr. Hollis' examinations are thorough, and they tell us a good deal about Pinter (his defense of Pinter against Robert Brustein's criticisms is particularly interesting), and a good deal about the modern theater. And he never gets away from his topic, Pinter's dramatic use of silence. He sees him as, among other things, a lyric poet whose "first obligation is to the how of communication and not to the what." He also points out that Pinter's prose, when spoken by trained actors acclimated to their parts, is far more exciting as it comes from the stage than when it is merely read. His language has always seemed to me (and this may be labeled heresy) to resemble, in effectiveness at least, some of the prose-fiction dialogues of the early (and best) Hemingway, which also had their compelling projections of silences.

It may be deduced from the foregoing—if not, the text of the book will soon make it evident—that James R. Hollis is the kind of critic sorely needed today: a technical critic. To speak of him in this way is not to suggest that he is unaware of such elements as the thematic (a brief acquaintance with his book will dispel any such notion), but it is to praise him for getting at the roots of these Pinter plays. Too many critics today are entirely philosophical, basing their "criticisms" exclusively on ideas, as if language differences between authors didn't matter—or, say, their ability to weld character into plot. To some of them, then, the concept of silence becomes a purely philosophical matter, with no relation to technique, to expression. In London a year or so ago I read (in either Encounter or the London Magazine) an essay in which an American-based critic dealt with the literature of silence without once even vaguely defining the literature of silence. Mr. Hollis doesn't give us this kind of treatment. He takes us into the living center of the present-day theater and shows us why, ideationally and technically, Harold Pinter is a significant dramatist.

HARRY T. MOORE

Southern Illinois University
April 26, 1970

Introduction

The community of scholarship permits dialogue between unseen colleagues and liberates one to focus on some particular perspective without feeling that other important considerations are being neglected. This present volume will not survey the entire Pinter corpus in detail but will rather educe the linguistic and metaphoric patterns of the major plays. Anyone interested, for example, in the radio, television, or film scripts, or in a chronological treatment of the corpus may profitably turn to Arnold Hinchliffe's *Harold Pinter* in the Twayne series.

Even though some of the groundwork has been laid by Mr. Hinchliffe's survey, this book is still influenced by the comparative obscurity of Pinter's work in America. Thus I have tried to do three things that would likely assist the general student of Pinter who has perhaps seen or read only a limited number of the plays. First, the Prologue surveys the cultural context in which Pinter works, the philosophical and theatrical currents, and the central focus of this particular study. Secondly, each discussion of a play includes an outline of the salient incidents of the play for those who have not seen or read it. These outlines do not attempt to retell the plot in its entirety but rather to make a knowledgeable discussion of the important movements of the play possible. Thirdly, all references and quotes from the plays will be noted parenthetically in the text and are based on the Grove Press paper editions, the editions most readily available to American readers. Exceptions include "The Examination" and the last two plays, *Landscape* and *Silence*, whose references are noted in the bibliography. It has been necessary to make a sizeable number of citations from the text since the particular flavor of Pinter's language, the concern of this study, can only be conveyed by letting the reader witness the phenomenon itself.

I should like to thank Mr. Harold Pinter, Grove Press, Methuen and Co., Ltd., and ACTAC (Theatrical and Cinematic) Ltd. for permission to quote from the plays. Also I should like to thank the library staff at Manchester College, Professor Henry Glade, and Miss Marcia Kump for their assistance in the preparation of this manuscript. Most of all, I want to acknowledge the sustaining graces of Bonnie, Taryn, and Timmy.

JAMES R. HOLLIS

Manchester College
Autumn 1969

Harold Pinter
The Poetics of Silence

Prologue

In the seventeenth century, that century so much like our own with its new science, its new theology, its new confidence, Blaise Pascal surveyed his age and concluded, "the eternal silence of these infinite spaces frightens me." In his own way Harold Pinter has listened to the labored pulse of his century, limned its temper, and perhaps more importantly, recreated its frightening silences. In a time which Tiutchev adumbrated as the "hour of wordless longing," Pinter serves us well by reminding us that we live in the space between words.

Perhaps man has always lived in the space between words, for it is the mysterious conspiracy between language and man which gives rise to the conception and embodiment of meaning. The motive of meaning is found precisely in man's impulse to overcome through language the apparent barrier between the outer and inner environments which he inhabits. When this chasm is spanned, outer and inner become synonymous. The outer world may continue to exist as matter apart from mind, but existentially it is experienced as inner. It may be true that there was a time when preconscious man moved between both worlds without differentiating between them, but the radical subjectivity of modern man betrays his effort to reestablish the original unity of mind and environment. The artist thus ministers to his culture when he fashions bridges (*meta pherein*) between outer and inner. An artist like Harold Pinter, for example, renders meaningful the awesome silences of this our space between words precisely by his metaphors of silence. When men and the language they use have a falling out, language paradoxically can only

1

be meaningful by revealing the meaninglessness of the occasion, the disintegration of the conspiracy.

If man has always lived in the space between words, he now lives in the space between Words as well. Albert Camus noted that the nineteenth century opened to the sound of falling ramparts. Standing amid the rubble of that century Matthew Arnold concluded, "There is not a creed which is not shaken, not an accredited dogma which is not shown to be questionable, not a received tradition which does not threaten to dissolve." He then went on to predict an immense destiny for poetry. Orthodoxy had attached its meaning to the fact and the authenticity of the fact had been undercut by diligent investigators such as Hennell, Strauss, Feuerbach, Lyell, Darwin, and Huxley. Art, however, because it attaches its meaning to the idea and not the fact, the linguistic concept and not its presumed referent, will thereby supplant religion as the repository of personal and cultural value. If Arnold's benediction over the still warm body of Christendom was premature, his point is nevertheless worth continued consideration.

If it is true that language is man's vehicle for the expression of the meaningful, then the artist whose gift is the gift of tongues will always help his contemporaries say what they long to say. This is not to contend that artists comprise the new priesthood while theologians are shuttled off into history's dusty attic. Nor is it to argue that religion and a number of other cultural institutions, rent as they are, have nothing further to offer man; obviously they do. It is rather to affirm that when one wishes to know what it means to be human on this spot at this time, he is well-advised to listen to those artists who seem to be expressing his deepest needs, his profoundest secrets. Like the slave of the *Meno* he may discover what is true for him by re-cognizing it, by realizing that he has only forgotten it and now requires some itinerant magician to speak the words that awaken the psyche from its slumber.

There are playwrights at work today who are attempting the radical recovery of language, the gift of tongues, the prophetic gesture, the celebration of sound and silence and whose work is thus, in the broadest sense, profoundly religious. Both the classical and the medieval dramatic traditions began in the spirit of wonder and, for all the agonies of modern drama, it is in wonderment that the artist writes again. With his predecessors the contemporary dramatist also writes knowing that he is not immortal, that all things are touched by the tick of time, that dust still "hath closed Helen's eye." He agrees with Yeats in "Nineteen Hundred and Nineteen" that

> Man is in love and loves what vanishes,
> What more is there to say?

yet he continues to write. Like his predecessors he knows that he is not omniscient and that subjectivity is his only course through a world of objects. Reason remains a clumsy and undependable tool in a thoroughly irrational world, a bludgeon in his hands when brain surgery is required. The aesthetic implications of such epistemological uncertainty are summarized by Pinter,

I suggest that there can be no hard distinctions between what is real and what is unreal, nor between what is true and what is false. A thing is not necessarily either true or false; it can be both true and false. A character on the stage who can present no convincing argument or information as to his past experience, his present behaviour or his aspirations, nor give a comprehensive analysis of his motives is as legitimate and as worthy of attention as one who, alarmingly, can do all these things. The more acute the experience the less articulate its expression.[1]

Furthermore, the contemporary playwright also creates without the unifying and stabilizing axiologies of the past. The exhaustion of past forms, even of Western humanism itself, has led us to the *Dies Irae* of our culture. As George Steiner remarks, "We know now that a man can read Goethe or Rilke in the evening, that he can play Bach and Schubert, and go to his day's work at Auschwitz in the morning."[2] Because of the collapse of external, unifying axiologies, man finds himself thrust radically back upon himself, condemned to the sundry solipsisms of what Hopkins might have called his "own sweating self."

The best of the modern dramatists continue to involve themselves in life, to celebrate the wondrous lineaments of man even though the shallow optimisms of earlier times have dissolved. The options open to characters who confront what Graham Greene called this "terrible, aboriginal tragedy" are obvious: suicide or accommodation. Often the crucial decision is made unconsciously, for there are as many forms of suicide as there are dead men who yet walk about. Similarly, there are many accommodations made with the dark, many fictions exalted to the status of reality. Pinter is one of a number of contemporary playwrights who is willing to probe the dark underside, to strip the napkins from the eyes of his characters. He is thus in a long tradition of the theatre, the tradition of that scabrous "old mole," Hamlet's father, who knocks about beneath the boards and reminds us that something is rotten after all.

While it is clearly dangerous to attempt to label and categorize different playwrights who are doing different things, still it may be useful to point out the affinities between a number of otherwise disparate authors in order to show the immediate dramatic context in which Pinter is working and from which he is departing. The most vital streams to emerge in the post World War II period include the so-called "theatre of the absurd" in Europe and America and the generation of "angry young men" in England. Martin Esslin's phrase, "theatre of the absurd," has been so influential as to virtually create a movement where only individuals worked before. Although Esslin has modified his stand in recent years he still, and rightly, argues for the usefulness of the term *absurd* as a point of entry into much of modern theatre. It is possible to make the definition of the "absurd" so broad as to include playwrights as diverse as Shakespeare and Adamov simply because some of their characters seem to be confronting the absurdity of their situation. But when we speak of the "theatre of absurd" today, we are rather speaking of a specific group whose philosophical allegiance may shift now and then but whose commitment is to a kind of theatre traditional in purpose but iconoclastic in form and temper.

The starting point for absurdist drama (and that of Pinter) is the relocation of meaning as a metaphysical category toward meaning as a complex of existentially experienced emotions such as dread, guilt, and uncertainty. Because of the virtual collapse of external frames of reference these emotions are not articulated in traditional formulations as sin, grace, or whatever, but as nameless and enigmatic currents within the spirit. This interiorization of modern literature may typically be witnessed in Dostoevski's underground man, in Rilke's comment in the seventh Duino elegy that "Nowhere . . . can world exist but within," and in the conversations of Pinter's characters which are in fact interior monologues shaped and tempered not by the subject at hand but by the demands of the spirit.[3] Frederick Hoffmann has observed, "characters who were formerly maneuvered within an accepted frame of extra-literary reference are now represented as seeking their own definitions and their own languages."[4] What needs to be added is that much of this groping for language (in Pinter's work especially) occurs at the unconscious level. The characters may be perfectly willing to offer rationalizations for their behavior, but unwittingly they betray their uncertainties and misgivings the more they expect their words to assist them.

Furthermore, the traditional categories of "tragedy," "comedy," and "tragi-comedy" are useless, for the absurdists mix them all into a witch's brew. Absurd drama may occasionally be tragic in the aristotelian sense, but it also goes beyond tragedy and beyond even the purgative laughter of the comic. Indeed the laughter which emerges from such theatre has a hollow ring, leading Guicharnaud to observe that "when we laugh at the farces of today, we are toppling over into the chasms of our own mouths."[5] Much of the laughter which one hears in Pinter's audiences seems a species of nervous laughter which releases tensions occasioned by characters becoming uncomfortably recognizable and situations unaccountably familiar.

Christopher Fry tells the story of a friend who, under the influence of a soporific, dreamed he was reading the book of life, a volume of alternating pages of comedy and tragedy. With growing excitement the friend hurried through the book to discover whether the conclusion was comic or tragic. Reaching the final page, he exploded in laughter, for the secret of life was comic. But when he tried to express the insights he had discovered, the words of that last page had fled him. It is interesting to speculate what an onlooker might have thought. Seeing the friend with tears of laughter streaming down his face and laboring vainly to speak, he might well have concluded that the friend was in the throes of the tragic *agon*. Similarly, it may be instructive to see that behind the twisted countenance, the labored articulation of much of modern drama, one may sometimes discern comic overtones. However, the comedy is experienced so intensely that the laughter it occasions may be mistaken for anguish.

While one may occasionally find modulations of tragedy and comedy in the work of Pinter and others, it is also clear that these terms are not very descriptive.[6] Tragedy and comedy arise out of a moral order that has been challenged in thought or act by hero or clown. The representatives of the theatre of the absurd affirm that the order is disordered and that one act has pretty much the moral stature of any other act; therefore it is futile to talk about *moral* order. Equally, one is uselessly employed in talking about *order* if every moment is isolated and discrete. But what of history, we say? What of memory? Do not the semanticists tell us how we bind the events of our collective lives together? But Apollonaire observed in "Cors de Chaisse" that "memory is a hunting horn whose sound dies out along the wind." Ionesco in *The Chairs,* Beckett in *Endgame,* or Pinter in *The Caretaker* depict their characters recollecting what happened in Paris in 1929 or in Luton some time back. But, practically speaking, there is no vital connection between what is happening now and what happened then. In effect the past is severed from the present and the acts of the present are severed from each other. Accordingly it is useless to talk of the tragic or comic vision of a playwright like Pinter, for he is operating with a different set of assumptions. Although the character of the metaphysical questions he is raising places him in the heritage of Sophocles and Aristophanes, he has in fact a different perspective founded on the denial of metaphysics and expressed in forms which preclude systems and, moreover, spend a good deal of time hacking the old systems to pieces. The point is not to reconstruct a system or to offer a new one. It is to demonstrate that metaphysical order, and therefore its byproducts comedy and tragedy, is no longer possible.

If there is any pattern which occurs repeatedly and characteristically in absurdist drama, it is the ironic. The ironic posture, "the dry mock," "the pathos of the middle," has three characteristics which are evident in the absurdist theatre.[7] First, the ironist is superior to that which he describes; that is, he is capable of rising above a situation in order to describe it. Secondly, the ironist exemplifies the Socratic stance which humbly confesses its ignorance and its impotence as a saving power. Thirdly, the ironist, for all his aesthetic distance, recognizes his own involvement in the human condition which he reflects. Thus the absurdist will not elaborate mythic structures which may have ministered to an earlier age but will rather express his own radical subjectivity. Accordingly, the metaphors of the absurdists simultaneously criticize and confess their implication in that which they criticize. One should not therefore seek an answer from an artist who is simply and honestly trying to find out what the questions are. As Pinter observed to an interviewer, "Whenever anything is answered simply, you must be asking the wrong question."[8] One should not expect of such an artist a vision of comic or tragic completion when his more immediate problem is to recover the possibilities of vision. Blake argued that the function of poetry is the recovery of paradise. Perhaps the task of the contemporary is the recovery of Blake, and thereby the recovery of a time when the word *paradise* may be spoken without embarrassment.

Dramatic irony emerges from the disparity between expectation and result. "The difference between expectation (seeming) and actual outcome (reality) is the pervading irony of Harold Pinter's work."[9] But Pinter's irony goes beyond "dramatic" or "Sophoclean" irony; it is existential irony. Pinter's plays may be ironic at many levels but their most pervasive irony arises from our confrontation with the world we actually live in but do not recognize. We ascribe anonymity to the characters and situations of Pinter's drama precisely because they are too familiar, too disconcertingly close to where we live. Most critics of Pinter have not traced his irony far enough. Pinter's rooms are ironic in the ordinary sense because they are more than rooms. Ruby Cohn notes how the rooms are naturalistically portrayed, "but by the end of each play, they become sealed containers, virtual coffins." [10] The deeper irony becomes apparent when we discover that the rooms which may be "coffins" are also, and finally, rooms. They are the rooms we live in. Thus, the audience is implicated in the irony of Pinter's work in a fashion which is not superficially apparent but which accounts for the discomfort heroes and heroines always feel at the moment of *anagnorisis*. Thus the deepest ironic intent of Pinter's work is to make strange that which is familiar and to make familiar that which is strange. Or as Stoppard's Guildenstern observes, "All your life you live so close to truth, it becomes a permanent blur in the corner of your eye, and when something nudges it into outline it is like being ambushed by a grotesque." [11]

Just as the invention of the daguerreotype ended the necessity for representational art so the experiments in expressionism and surrealism earlier in this century freed the absurdists from the traditional mimetic and realistic assumptions of Western theatre. This freedom has occasioned expressionistic extravaganzas beginning with Jarry's *Ubu Roi* and perhaps culminating with Ionesco's *Rhinoceros*, Beckett's *Play*, or even *Hair*. But even though Pinter's plays often seem bizzare and rather mysterious, they are nevertheless overtly realistic in their mood and movements. His characters, for example, are clearly upper, middle, or working-class types although that is not to say that they are typological or allegorical. Even though the problems of any single character may be paradigmatic, they are also distinctly individual. Pinter's characters are not pasteboard figures demanding a one-to-one identification with some allegorical backdrop; rather, they are open and incomplete as all men are open and incomplete. The abyss over which they seem to teeter is surely the same abyss which Heidegger describes as "the

openness of Being." Pinter does not dehumanize his characters as Beckett and Ionesco sometimes do; they remain
"human, all-too-human."

The absurdist point has been made repeatedly and the
playwright ill serves his culture or his muse if he continues to
make the same old point in the same old way. Furthermore,
through his abandonment of realism the absurdist often
lessens the apologetic success of his argument, precisely because the "realistic" world is the world his audience thinks it
lives in. It may be quite true that the world is surreal or, as
Borges would have it, not real at all. But most audiences, out
of some collective need, demand that the play be a familiar if
not slavish reproduction of what they think the world looks
like. If the absurdist wishes to make his case more effectively,
then, he may well wish to adopt a realistic or quasi-realistic
mode of presentation. His apologetic then will advance by
way of what Kierkegaard called "thoughts which wound
from behind." Pinter seems to be the only playwright to fuse
the absurdist consciousness with overtly conventional realism
to achieve a dramatically viable amalgam. In A *Slight Ache,*
for example, the audience readily enters into the world of the
play because it seems comfortably familiar. Soon they realize
themselves caught as the wasp is caught in the marmalade
and, having committed themselves, must wait upon the conclusion. Then the playwright has his audience from the
outset and they must see the matter through. Thus the
afternoon tea becomes a horrifying ritual of divestiture without ceasing to be an afternoon tea as well.

In *The Theatre of Protest and Paradox* George Wellwarth
argues that Pinter is not a creator but an eclectic scholar who
is well-read in the continental masters such as Beckett, Ionesco, Genet, and so on.[12] But Pinter is an original and
creative talent. It is true that he has imbibed the vapors of
the "masters," and it is true that they have informed his
vision, but the vision was there in the beginning. In fact,
Pinter is repeatedly surprised to learn that he is being compared with an author he has never read. He has explained
that his primary reading has been the novels of Hemingway,
Dostoevski, Joyce, Henry Miller, Kafka, and Beckett. He had

not read the plays of Ionesco, for example, until after some of his own plays were compared with those of Ionesco.[13] Pinter is not then an absurdist in the strictest sense although he seems to be doing many things that the absurdists are doing. There are points of influence perhaps, but Pinter's voice is distinct and individual.

Just as a playwright may respond to the tenor of his times so he may also contribute or magnify the tendencies of those times in his work. The absurdists, for example, have attuned us to the bankruptcy of many of our institutions and have in turn helped create an atmosphere in which those institutions seem even less viable. Pinter also began his career in an atmosphere disturbed by the generation of so-called "angry young men." Nothing much besides the verse drama of Eliot and Fry and the usual commercial froth had come out of England since World War II until that May of 1956 when John Osborne's *Look Back in Anger* exploded and changed the course of English theatre. Osborne articulated the uneasy sense of the average Englishman that things had changed, that the sun had finally set on the Empire, that the old values of class and crown were hollow and insipid. Pascal's comment that "we wander in times which are not ours" seemed to describe the cultural malaise that Jimmy Porter and his fellows echoed. Alison, Jimmy's wife, tells her father,

You're hurt because everything is changed. Jimmy is hurt because everything is the same. And neither of you can face it. Something's gone wrong somewhere, hasn't it?

Or, as Frank Norman's title so aptly expressed, *Fings Ain't Wot They Used T'be.*

Part of this malaise was unique to the last outposts of European imperialism, but part of the uneasiness originated in the growing recognition that the entire world had gotten out of hand, that the energies of destruction were implacable. Jimmy Porter explained,

There aren't any good, brave causes left. If the big bang does come, and we all get killed off, it won't be in aid of the old-fashioned, grand design. It'll just be for the Brave New-nothing-very-much-thank-you. About as pointless and inglorious as stepping in front of a bus.

Osborne's play, important in itself, is even more important for its role in reviving the vitality of the English stage. Almost overnight a host of new playwrights emerged. While it is not useful to discuss their individual contributions here, a mere listing of names now familiar to American and continental audiences reveals the breadth and intensity of the revival—Ann Jellicoe, N. F. Simpson, Brendan Behan, Shelagh Delaney, John Arden, Arnold Wesker, Alun Owen, Tom Stoppard, and Harold Pinter. There are many others who might be mentioned but the point is obvious. Osborne had somehow tapped a reservoir of emotions ranging from anger and hostility to profound anxiety and sadness.

Novelist Allan Sillitoe recalls how he "happened to see a performance of *Look Back in Anger*—in Brighton of all places, where the reaction of one middle-aged middle-class woman after the first act was: 'But people just don't live like that.' Jimmy Porter's shrapnel bombs were bursting with marvellous accuracy above the neatly stacked sandbags of Coward and Rattigan. I knew that the frontier was wide open. . . ." [14]

All of the playwrights were young. Born between the wars, they initially responded to the atmosphere of "*entre deux guerres*," of "wandering between two worlds, one dead, the other powerless to be born" with rage and indignation. But a decade later it is very difficult to trace the development of their energies, for they have ranged from naturalism to epic theatre to the absurd and back again. Perhaps it is only judicious to observe the enormous vitality of the decade in which Pinter began writing. A century earlier Arnold had observed in "The Function of Criticism Today" that it is necessary for an artist to inherit an atmosphere alive with ideas and the willingness to experiment. In a period of creative dearth the critic best serves art by promoting and circulating the best that has been thought and said until the sense of culture revives and the artist is recalled to his labors. Whether or not Arnold's thesis is valid may be debated, but it is clear that after a period of dearth, the English dramatic impulse had been recharged and Pinter found himself in its midst.

Harold Pinter was just twenty-six when Jimmy Porter said

for the first time, "Why do I do this every Sunday? Even the book reviews seem to be the same as last week's. Different books—same reviews." Pinter was then at the right place at the right time; and while it is not accurate to talk of Pinter as an "absurdist" or as an "angry young man," it is true to say that his technique and consciousness were influenced by the atmosphere both forces generated.

While the concern of this study is not biographical, it may be of some use to briefly rehearse the salient features of Pinter's life that we may better understand his work in a context. He was born in London on 10 October 1930, to Hyman and Frances Pinter. Mr. Pinter was a tailor in London's East End, a neighborhood comparable to New York's Lower East Side. The Pinters were of the Jewish tradition and had migrated to London from Eastern Europe. Between 1941 and 1947 Harold Pinter attended London's Hackney Downs Grammar School where his acting ability in school plays was sufficiently recognized that he was encouraged to pursue an acting career. Accordingly he enrolled at the Royal Academy of Dramatic Art in 1948 where his aversion to "a terrible atmosphere of affectation and unreality, ankle bands and golden hair" led him to join a traveling repertory company the following year. For the next decade, under his stage name David Baron, Pinter traveled the English and Irish provinces acting in Shakespearean and contemporary roles. Something of the flavor of those years when Pinter was about the learning of his craft is suggested by his 1968 MAC, an affectionate memoir of the Irish player-manager Anew McMaster in whose company he traveled.

Ever since grammar school Pinter had been writing verse or short dramatic sketches and started but did not finish a novel titled The Dwarfs. (The Dwarfs was ultimately transformed into a radio play which was first broadcast in 1960.) In a 1960 interview with Kenneth Tynan on the BBC, Pinter explained the circumstances under which he wrote his first play, The Room. He had mentioned his idea for a play to a friend at Bristol University. Shortly thereafter the friend replied saying that if Pinter wanted his play performed he would have to forward the manuscript within a week. "So I wrote back," Pinter related, "and told him to forget about the whole thing. And then I sat down and wrote it in four days. I don't quite know how it happened, but it did." [15] Seldom is there anything in biography to explain why a writer works the way he does. Pinter even suggests that the biography itself may be in doubt. "I had—I have—nothing to say about myself, directly. I wouldn't know where to begin. Particularly since I often look at myself in the mirror and say, 'who the hell's that?' " [16]

Before turning to the discussion of the first group of plays, it seems germane to introduce the primary focus of this study. There are multiple foci that can be and often are examined in the following survey, but the single issue which every student of Pinter must confront is the playwright's relationship to and utilization of language. One of the central tenets of the absurdists is the breakdown, even the impossibility, of communication in our time. Ionesco reduces this complex phenomenon to a simple conclusion, "I detect a crisis of thought, which is manifested by a crisis of language; words no longer meaning anything." This distrust of language has often led to the acting out of the drama's metaphors and the replacement of traditional rhetoric by the language of gesture. In its most radical form the language of gesture may be seen in the mimes, parodies, and charades of Beckett. Pinter perceives similar problems of communication as Beckett but employs a different strategy of dramatization.

Pinter employs language to describe the failure of language; he details in forms abundant the poverty of man's communication; he assembles words to remind us that we live in the space between words. When asked why he thought conversations were so crucial to the success of his plays, Pinter replied, "I don't know, I think possibly it's because people fall back on anything they can lay their hands on verbally to keep away from the danger of knowing, and of being known." [17] The effect of Pinter's language, then, is to note that the most important things are not being said, that the dove that would descend to speak the procreative word still hovers amid the precincts of silence.

Although Eric Bentley's dictum that "a drama not verbalized is a drama not dramatized" [18] must be tempered by our recognition that the drama may also communicate through the language of gesture, the special role of language in some form is obviously necessary to the drama. At the same time we recognize that language is an inadequate vehicle to communicate all that we would desire. For, as Flaubert observed in *Madame Bovary*, "human speech is like a cracked kettle on which we tap crude rhythms for bears to dance to, while we long to make music that will melt the stars."

Thus we find those occasions where we reach the end of language, when we stand as on a pier wondering how we may get ourselves across to the other side when we have no vessel to support us. On those occasions we may vent our frustration in rage or malice or self-pity until we recognize the irony in cursing language itself and we grow silent. As the British psychiatrist Laing observes.

At the point of nonbeing we are at the outer reaches of what language can state, but we can indicate by language why language cannot say what it cannot say. I cannot say what cannot be said, but sounds can make us listen to the silence. Within the confines of language it is possible to indicate when the dots must begin. . . . But language can be used to convey what it cannot say—by its interstices, by its emptiness and lapses, by the latticework of words, syntax, sound and meanings. The modulations of pitch and volume delineate the form precisely by not filling in the spaces between the lines. But it is a grave mistake to take the lines for the pattern, or the pattern for that which it is patterning.[19]

It is our silence, then, that speaks more eloquently of our condition than we could possibly express otherwise.

Language is obviously important in Pinter's effort to get himself across to us, but we must also recognize the many occasions when it is through silence that he communicates. There are many ways in which Pinter uses silence to articulate, but the first, and perhaps most common, is simply *the pause*. The pause occurs when the character has said what he has to say and is waiting for a response from the other side, or it occurs when he cannot find the words to say what he wants to say. In either case he has attempted to span the

chasm that exists between him and those around him. He is
caught up short; he has reached the limits of language and
now waits in silence for something to happen.

There are other occasions in the plays of Pinter when the
silence is hard to hear because there are so many sounds
being made at the same time. It is not uncommon today to
see people walking down the street with transistor radios in
their pockets. They, having heard the terrible silence of these
infinite spaces, desire to surround themselves with sound,
sound which comforts and sustains by promising companion-
ship and advertising that there really is a fixed world out
there which somebody, every hour on the hour, reassures
them is running according to schedule.

In *The Red and the Black* Stendhal observed that "man
was gifted with speech to help him conceal his thoughts." So
much of the sound which surrounds us today is the product
of our existential anxieties and represents our refusal to
accept the consequences of our finitude and our isolation.
This is the silence which lies behind language and which
always threatens to break into our conversations in embar-
rassing ways. This is the silence which is most evident when
the world is at its noisiest. This is *the silence which emerges
when the most important things are left unsaid*. Pinter has
observed of our condition,

There are two silences. One when no word is spoken. The other
when perhaps a torrent of language is being employed. This
speech is speaking of a language locked beneath it. That is its
continual reference. The speech we hear is an indication of that
which we don't hear. It is a necessary avoidance, a violent, sly,
anguished or mocking smoke screen which keeps the other in its
place. When true silence falls we are still left with echo but are
nearer nakedness. One way of looking at speech is to say that it
is a constant stratagem to cover nakedness.[20]

A different though not unrelated kind of silence is discovered in the emptiness of that language which we do use. If
language is to be the vehicle of the self's expression, we must
conclude that the inane chatter which now seems so common exposes the poverty of the modern self. Writing in *Past
and Present* Thomas Carlyle observed a century ago:

Insincere Speech, truly, is the prime material of insincere Action. Action hangs, as it were, *dissolved* in Speech, in Thought whereof Speech is the shadow; and precipitates itself therefrom. The kind of Speech in a man betokens the kind of Action you will get from him. Our Speech, in these modern days, has become amazing.

If the fulminating Carlyle but knew the further occasions in which the resources of language, and therefore of the self, might be exhausted he might well have dissolved in a puff of apocalyptic smoke.

Pinter's characters typically manifest the exhaustion of their capacities and of the forms by which they live. Although they may fill the air with words, *the silence of these characters is the result of their having nothing to say.* Ionesco has effectively parodied this cultural phenomenon by eliciting nonsense syllables from his characters. Pinter has tried to do the same thing the hard way, that is by using the normal speech of the characters to reveal the poverty, the emptiness of their lives. These are characters who finally exercise their power of speech but find themselves, like the orator in Ionesco's *The Chairs*, filling the air with gibberish to camouflage the fact that they have nothing important to say.

There is, last, a species of silence that must be considered procreative in character and which can rarely be observed in the Pinter corpus. This silence is the result of a character's *anagnorisis* or insight into the nature of some supra-personal reality. It is comparable to the central ineffability of the mystical experience in which the character attains the consciousness of unity with the "Other." It is the outward manifestation of the inner *kenosis*, the emptying of the self into the larger non-self. This emptying is not the occasion of emptiness but the experience of fullness. It is the occasion of silence to which one is moved when he feels an identity with something outside himself, something infinite which is available to those finite. It is the reverence of the child in the presence of a rite which he does not understand. It is the silence of the priest before he lifts the host. It is *the silence which is our homage to being, to the totality of what is* although we do not know it in its entirety nor even necessarily approve of it. It is that act whereby we willingly lay aside that which makes us most human, language, as a sign of our wonder at the more than human.

When we consider the Pinter corpus, we find that much of what he is doing was in some way anticipated by the absurdists in their exposure of the exhaustion of language and the consequent breakdown of communication and by the angry young men who tried to accurately record the conversations they heard in order to hold them up for our critical scrutiny. Even Pinter's apparent discovery of the dramatic value of silence may in some sense be derived. Certainly one of the influences of Beckett on Pinter is his use of silence. Beckett strategically scatters pauses throughout his plays when the characters seem brought up short by the implications of the language they use. As a character in Beckett's *Endgame* muses,

> I use the words you taught me. If they don't mean anything anymore, teach me others. Or let me be silent.

Pinter begins at this point of exhaustion and in his form and fashion forges a new poetic, a poetic of silence.

The etymology of the word *poetry* (*poiein*, maker) is instructive, for we can observe in the plays of Pinter occasions where he has "made" silence, that is, given it "a local habitation and a name." Silence is more than an absence and Pinter's gift has been to create dramatic representations of silence as a presence. In *Symbols of Transformation* Jung observes that language never loses "its synomic or dual reference; its meaning is both personal and social." [21] A comparable observation should be made of silence. The silent structures which the characters of Pinter have fashioned for themselves are not unlike those which the rest of us frequent. While there is much in Pinter which is of significance to the discerning observer of contemporary artistic expression, perhaps nothing is more important than Pinter's endeavor to forge a poetic out of the silence which surrounds us.

1

The Room as Metaphor
The Room, The Birthday Party, The Dumb Waiter

If it is true that we live in the space between words, a time when the word unheard supplants the word misunderstood, then the task of the artist is to resume the ancient calling of poet and prophet (*vates*). As prophet he may only be able to proclaim the hour of death, for, as Kierkegaard noted in 1849, sometimes a man cannot save his age—he can only express his certainty that it will perish. But as a poet the contemporary artist has a more immediate service to render. As a poet he is acquainted with the broad range of nondiscursive modes of expression which are still available to the imaginative man. These modes make it possible to go beyond rational discourse to articulate the prodigious spaces and thunderous silences of this age. Among the modes of expression open to the artist who seeks to go beyond the merely logical and definitional, who seeks to span the gulf which daily grows between man and the receding tide of meaning the most important is metaphor.

The aesthetic consciousness is perhaps best characterized by a heightened sensitivity to the hidden relationship between apparently dissimilar things. Such a consciousness is "metaphoric" inasmuch as it establishes points of reference unavailable to a purely logical framework for comparison. By way of metaphor, then, the poet is able to incorporate the external world into his own in a fashion qualitatively different from the cognitive processes of most other men. The outer world is interiorized and becomes, in Rilke's term, for example, a *Weltinnenraum*.

This capacity for interiorization is the basic epistemological strategy of cognitive man. But the interiorizing faculty of the artist is also accompanied by an externalizing process whereby the inner world is re-presented as consciousness. One of the means by which the artist retranslates his internalized experience is metaphor. In the playwright, as in other men, the world of external experience is assimilated into the unconscious. The playwright's task, however, is to find dramatically viable metaphors for the re-presentation and recovery of experience. *Metaphor, therefore, is a vehicle for the repristination of experience.* Thus, when we see the play and permit its metaphors to work on our consciousness we open the possibility of communication, of shared experience even though the radical isolation of the individual seems to preclude meaningful contact with others. We find, then, that the metaphors of a playwright like Pinter go a long way toward making meaningful conversation possible again even though his strategy may involve frightening lapses of conversation.

Through a recovery of metaphor we come to an understanding of how the individual artist may best minister to his age while speaking to it in the most oblique fashion. For example, the tangled course of man's relationship to his environment may be broadly traced through the nineteenth century by observing the gradual shift in metaphoric emphasis from the naturalistic metaphors of a Wordsworth who saw a force that rolled through all things to the mechanistic metaphors of the Victorians. The further dissolution of societal ties intensified the isolation of man within the city and increased his estrangement not only from his natural roots but from his fellows. One of the central metaphors in Pinter is "the room." The room is suggestive of the encapsulated environment of modern man, but may also suggest something of his regressive aversion to the hostile world outside. The dogma of regression to the womb is overused, but the events of this century provide ample evidence that there are comparable atavistic affects and motives which insistently demand their expression.[1]

Perhaps the greatest dilemma of the student of Pinter is to

know how far he ought to ride with the metaphor. To say that Pinter's metaphors have multiple possibilities is not to blunder into a naïve confusion of the critic's ingenuity with the author's confessed purpose in the play. Rather, to argue for a multiplicity of meanings is to permit the metaphors to remain open-ended, to point beyond themselves to the rich and variegated texture of that experience which they repristinate.

The observer of Pinter's plays discovers all sorts of "eyes that peep with a familiar gleam" from what Baudelaire called the symbolic wood. The discussions which follow assemble a number of metaphoric foci which emerge without necessarily trying to tie them down to a fixed and consistent framework. Susan Sontag has concluded,

In most modern instances, interpretation amounts to the philistine refusal to leave the work of art alone. Real art has the capacity to make us nervous. By reducing the work of art to its content and then interpreting that, one tames the work of art. Interpretation makes art manageable, conformable.[2]

Hopefully these discussions will recreate some of the echoes which reverberate behind the flats, recover some of the hidden gestures, and return us to the primary experience of the play itself.

The Room (1957), Pinter's first play, is about two people in a room. However much one would wish to embellish the business, the play is finally about two people in a room. Pinter had been playing Rochester and Vivien Merchant, his wife-to-be, Jane Eyre in the Bournemouth Repertory Company when he went into a room on the tour and saw two men. One was a small barefooted man and the other was a large lorry driver. The little man talked and fed the other who remained silent. This odd but hardly mysterious scene became a compelling image which Pinter felt he had to give dramatic embodiment.

I went into a room one day and saw a couple of people in it. This stuck with me for some time afterwards, and I felt that the only way I could give it expression and get it off my mind was dramatically. I started off with this picture of the two people and let them carry on from there.[3]

In the course of *The Room* the lorry driver Pinter had seen remains a silent, morose lorry driver named Bert Hudd, and the small man is transformed into Bert's garrulous wife Rose.

The setting in which Rose and Bert find themselves is not abstract but intensely concrete. Things are things and not signs or symbols pointing beyond the clutter to something else. Perhaps because our experience of the theatre leads us to expect a door to be something other than or in addition to a door, we are vaguely discomfited. A door which does not explain itself or from which we expect some kind of explanation becomes mysterious, even ominous. It seems absurd to think of a door as ominous, but we find ourselves wondering if someone will knock on the door, come in, and make demands of us. In a 1960 BBC interview Kenneth Tynan asked Pinter what the people in the room were afraid of and Pinter replied, "Obviously they are scared of what is outside the room. Outside the room there is a world bearing upon them which is frightening. I am sure it is frightening to you and me as well." Thus concrete things, without ceasing to be things, become charged with subconscious wishes and fears. Without ceasing to be a thing, the door becomes an extension of one's identity as well. *The Room*, then, is about two people in a room and how they invest that room with the secrets of their concealed lives.

Bert sits at the table eating breakfast and reading a magazine while Rose hovers about him, feeding him, reprimanding him, advising him, imploring him. She says to him as she feeds him, "Here you are. This'll keep the cold out." "It's very cold out; I can tell you. It's murder." "Still, the room keeps warm. It's better than the basement, anyway" (95). Bert says nothing. Rose continues to discuss the weather and, without overtly reintroducing the topic of the basement, observes, "I've never seen who it is. Who is it? Who lives down there? I'll have to ask. I mean, you might as well know, Bert. But whoever it is, it can't be too cosy" (96). Bert is silent.

Bert's reticence is superficially humorous to the audience, but it is horrifying to Rose. His silence is the silence of one who has nothing to say while her loquacity is the silence of one who is trying desperately but failing to say what she really wants to say. She really wants to say that she is afraid of the cold, of the night, and of the tenebrific forces that may lurk in the basement. She is asking Bert to respond to her needs, to bring her warmth, and to accept her hesitant overtures of love. But Bert is silent. While Rose fantasizes about the loving family circle of which she is the center, her mind returns to the basement, and she concludes that maybe "foreigners" are living down there. Her fear of aliens is common to a number of Pinter's characters, notably Davies in *The Caretaker*. Aliens threaten to break into the shell one has constructed and are therefore regarded with fear and suspicion. Rose's mind shifts back and forth between the security of her room and the strangers below. "This is a good room. You've got a chance in a place like this. . . . I wonder who has got it now. I've never seen them, or heard of them. But I think someone's down there" (99).

In the midst of this talk of strangers "down there," someone knocks on the door. It is the caretaker, Mr. Kidd, who, having entered, announces "I knocked." The ominous threat is materialized as a harmless old duffer who, though he is the caretaker, is no longer certain how many floors there are in the house or who else lives there. When asked about his family who are all now dead, he replies after a pause that he "makes ends meet."

    [*pause*]
ROSE   You full at the moment, Mr. Kidd?
MR. KIDD   Packed out.
ROSE   All sorts, I suppose?
MR. KIDD   Oh yes, I make ends meet.
ROSE   We do, too, don't we, Bert?
    [*pause*] (103)

From the dross of working-class speech Pinter refines a poetic dialogue that lifts, and sways, and returns to the starting point. The exchange seems innocent but the tenor and tempo reveal the larger gestures behind, the accommodations with darkness which language is called upon to cover.

Finally it is time for Bert to leave on a run that he is making. Rose dresses him and he departs without having said a word. Rose is now alone in the room. She looks about the room, unable to substitute the clutter of the room for the emptiness of her situation. She casually opens the door and is terrified to see two people standing there, Mr. and Mrs. Sands who have come to enquire about a room. Mrs. Sands observes, "You know, this is a room you can sit down and feel cosy in" (106). A moment later she observes,

> It's very dark out.
> MR. SANDS   No darker than in.
> MRS. SANDS   He's right there.
> MR. SANDS   It's darker in than out, for my money. (107)

Finally Rose interrupts, "I never go out at night. We stay in." She explains how she stays in her room and does not venture out and, inadvertently, bother someone. Her unspoken wish is that likewise no one should bother her.

In the course of her conversation with the Sands, Rose learns that they have just come from the basement where they met a man who was living there. Rose admits that once, a long time ago, she had been in the basement and now she earnestly inquires of the stranger below. But the Sands get into a silly argument about whether Mr. Sands sat down or merely "perched." The argument is inappropriate to Rose's situation and only serves to delay their answers to the questions which she has about the stranger below. Finally the Sands explain that in the dark basement they confronted a man whom they could not see but who told them that a room upstairs, number seven, was indeed vacant. Rose lives in room number seven. "That's this room!" Rose exclaims. "This room is occupied" (112).

After the Sands have left Rose confronts Mr. Kidd.

> ROSE   Mr. Kidd, what did they mean about this room?
> MR. KIDD   What room?
> ROSE   Is this room vacant?
> MR. KIDD   Vacant?

ROSE They were looking for the landlord.

MR. KIDD Who were?

ROSE Listen, Mr. Kidd, you are the landlord, aren't you? There isn't any other landlord?

MR. KIDD What? What's that got to do with it? I don't know what you're talking about. I've got to tell you. I've had a terrible week-end. You'll have to see him. I can't take it any more. You've got to see him.
[pause]

ROSE Who? (113)

Rose's conversation betrays her anxiety. Again she does not say what she is really saying. She does not express her fears of being rooted out, of being supplanted from her cosy, womb-like room. The landlord not only does not speak to these questions but, further, seems to introduce the agent of her removal. The man in the basement, the alien, the voice in the darkness has been waiting for some time to see her. Rose disclaims knowledge of the stranger but Mr. Kidd observes that they must know each other.

The ambivalence of Rose's attitude toward the man in the cellar intensifies. She fears him and yet she seems drawn to acknowledge his presence. The shuttling back and forth in her mind becomes apparent when Mr. Kidd opines that the stranger will not leave after coming all this way.

ROSE All this way?

MR. KIDD You don't think he's going to do that, do you?
[pause]

ROSE He wouldn't do that.

MR. KIDD Oh yes. I know it.
[pause]

ROSE What's the time?

MR. KIDD I don't know.
[pause]

ROSE Fetch him. Quick. Quick! (116)

She seems worried that her husband will catch her with a male stranger, a rather humorous worry for a woman who is cast in her sixties. But more importantly, she seems drawn to confront that which threatens her, to meet this stranger who says he knows her and who has declared her room vacant.

And so she, like Faust with the poodle, decides to invite the darkness into her narrow circle of light.

The darkness seems doubly personified in the entrance of a blind Negro. Rose's reception is hardly cordial.

> I'm one ahead of people like you. Tell me what you want and get out.
>
> RILEY   My name is Riley.
>
> ROSE   I don't care if it's—what? That's not your name. That's not your name. You've got a grown-up woman in this room, do you hear? Or are you deaf too? You're not deaf too, are you? You're all deaf and dumb and blind, the lot of you. A bunch of cripples.
>
> RILEY   This is a large room.
>
> ROSE   Never mind about the room. What do you know about this room? You know nothing about it. And you won't be staying in it long either. . . . (116)

When talking with the Sands earlier, Rose indicated that she knew someone was down there but that she did not know his name. Now when the stranger tells her his name, she declares that he is not really "Riley." How does Rose know that he is not "Riley" unless she somehow already knows this stranger or, more likely, does not want to affix a name to that which should remain nameless?

Surprisingly one almost feels let down by the entrance of the blind Negro. It is true that he adds a further bit of mystification to a plot which is probably already mysterious enough; it is true that he is not an artificial *deux ex machina* because the threads of the plot are still left unwound; but it is also true that he represents an object upon which Rose's unnameable anxieties can be fixed and localized. Objections to Riley are minor, however, for the play succeeds in spite of his rather artificial entrance. Nevertheless, Rose (and the audience) has in Riley an object upon which the tensions generated by the play can be directed. *Angst* is denominated by its free-floating character, its resistance to our efforts to name, identify, or locate it. With Riley's entrance the anxiety becomes less general and, therefore, less pervasive; the movement, then, is from *Angst* toward fear. Fear may be grappled with but *Angst* always lies beyond one's grasp. To catch and hold the forever elusive is the dilemma of Rose and those of her species.

Riley tells Rose that he has a message for her, that her father wants her to come home. He calls Rose "Sal" and implores her to come home. The test of wills emerges in their stichomythic exchange.

RILEY   Come home, Sal.
ROSE   Don't call me that.
RILEY   Come, now.
ROSE   Don't call me that.
RILEY   So now you're here.
ROSE   Not Sal.
RILEY   Now I touch you.
ROSE   Don't touch me.
RILEY   Sal.
ROSE   I can't.
RILEY   I want you to come home.
ROSE   No.
RILEY   With me.
ROSE   I can't.
RILEY   I waited to see you.
ROSE   Yes.
RILEY   Now I see you.
ROSE   Yes.
RILEY   Sal.
ROSE   Not that.
RILEY   So, now.
        [pause]
        So, now.
ROSE   I've been here.
RILEY   Yes.
ROSE   Long.
RILEY   Yes.
ROSE   The day is a hump. I never go out.
RILEY   No.
ROSE   I've been here.
RILEY   Come home now, Sal. (118, 119)

Ever so slightly and subtly she is drawn toward Riley and finally reaches up and tenderly touches his eyes, the back of his head, and his temples, gestures which prefigure her own blindness.

In the midst of their groping embrace, Bert enters and draws the curtain, apparently to keep the outside outside. He describes his run with the van to Rose in vaguely sexual terms. Tooling up and down the intertwining network of roads, he lavishes on the feminine van the affection that he denies Rose.

> She was good. She went with me. She don't mix it with me. I use my hand. Like that. I get hold of her. I go where I go. She took me there. She brought me back.
> [*pause*]
> I got back all right. (120)

Then Bert notices Riley in the room and beats him viciously. The play ends with Rose clutching her eyes and crying that she cannot see.

The most immediate temptation is to allegorize *The Room*, to move the characters across a black and white grid and force them to conform to consistent patterns. Some critics have seen Riley, for example, as a rather trite image of Death who has come to call a reluctant Rose "home." Some see Riley as merely an unspecified past which has now come to haunt her and call her by the name which she has tried to forget. Perhaps the clumsiest effort to allegorize *The Room* is evidenced by the suggestion that Riley terrifies Rose so much because he reminds her that she has Negro blood in her veins, that her heritage is mixed with that of the aliens she fears. In all these suggestions Bert's role would seem that of a stupid and brutal husband who is nevertheless trying to shield his wife from the powers of darkness.

It is appropriate to observe without risking allegory that Rose's relationship to the room is crucial. The room is her refuge from whatever it is that she fears. It is light and warm inside and dark and cold outside. She clings to this warmth and fears that someone will open the door and let the darkness in. One commentator has generalized, "A Pinter play is always an X-ray touched up to suggest it is a snapshot, and its details reveal the desperate struggle of the organism to eject deadly bacteria." [4]

Rose knows that some one or some thing lurks out there and threatens her secure home. Indeed, something out there is calling to her and while she would reject its entreaty, Riley's entrance materializes all of the anxieties that beset her. Riley is really not his name, she thinks, because her deepest dread cannot be named.[5] Riley is familiar to her not because he is her father, or a kinsman, or Death, or the past, but because she has always lived for that moment when her dread might take shape and stand as a living thing before her. The confrontation with Riley is the re-cognition of that which she, like the slave of the *Meno*, has always known. In a previous discussion with the landlord on the subject of a familiar rocking chair, we find a prefiguration of Rose's own *anagnorisis*.

MR. KIDD   I seem to have some remembrance.
ROSE   It's just an old rocking-chair.
MR. KIDD   Was it here when you came?
ROSE   No, I brought it myself.
MR. KIDD   I could swear blind I've seen that before.
ROSE   Perhaps you have.
MR. KIDD   What?
ROSE   I say, perhaps you have.
MR. KIDD   Yes, maybe I have.
ROSE   Take a seat, Mr. Kidd.
MR. KIDD   I wouldn't take an oath on it though. (100, 101)

Riley asks her to come home with him. He asks her to take on the deepest knowledge of the self and recover her roots; but her potential homecoming, the psychic return to where she has always lived is aborted by Bert. Whether or not Rose would really have ventured out into the darkness to deal with the demons which she dreads one can never know. It is clear that the call to return to her "real" home is a threat to this room which she has fortified with the name "home." Her anxieties are translated into the only language the taciturn Bert knows—violence, and her isolation is confirmed and compounded by her blindness at the end.

There are some who will criticize Pinter for his clumsy conjuring in *The Room*. They will say that Rose would not succumb to Riley so easily, that no sane person would react as Rose and Bert to this harmless intruder. But these critics demand rational behavior in an irrational world; they succeed by sundry sophistries in rationalizing their own dread by means unavailable to a person like Rose. There is, for example, a cleaning lady in a midwestern library who, seeing a few scratches on a table, observed solemnly that the student who made those scratches was Communist inspired. The mechanism by which she was able to invest a furrow in a table with the conspiracies of her fears is the same mechanism that permits Rose to see in the blind Negro the embodiment of her existential anxiety. For to paraphrase Voltaire, if blind Negroes and Communists did not exist, they would have to be invented.

The easiest dodge of the critics in confronting the obscurities and contradictions of Pinter's plays is to say that they but mirror the confusions of our age. But such an explanation merely attempts to make uncertainty certain. Perhaps it is more accurate to say that Pinter's dramatized metaphors partake of that reality which logic-driven moderns deny in their effort to fix upon absolutes. Mrs. Hudd lives in the room, but the Sands are accurate in thinking the room empty. In *Right You Are, If You Think You Are* Pirandello resolves such a paradox by having his persona Laudisi conclude each act with a laugh, the quest for certainty concluding with an embrace of the opposites. Experience reminds us that contraries are true all the time. Metaphor is the discourse of divided experience, the schizophrenic in the asylum of language. Some regard Pinter's metaphors of contradiction and conclude, "that way lies madness." But others hear resonances from the deepest chords of their being, and admit that the anxieties of Rose take on the alarming posture of their own. Pinter, like Blake, would have us evade "Single vision & Newton's sleep."

The Room conveys a drab lower-class environment without the implicit sentimentalism of social reformers. This is not to say that Pinter is insensitive to the condition of his characters but that their psychological peril is his focus rather than their social deprivation. Thus the social environment is supplanted by the psychological environment and the psychological environment is the product of the needs and weaknesses of those characters. In Kenneth Burke's terms, the agents create the scene rather than the scene determining the agents as in most social drama. Pinter's characters are often the derelicts of the Welfare State who are concerned with "getting on," but their corporeal form seems little more than a temporary guise which their psychological natures have assumed.

As much as the barrenness of the room, the entry of Riley, the violence of Bert may contribute to the metaphoric atmosphere of the play, it is clear that language is the means through which Pinter articulates the nameless and says what one finds hard to say. Through his uncanny ear for the syntax and rhythms of common English speech, Pinter is able to reproduce the sundry kinds of silence which we often do not consciously hear. In *The Black and White* (1959), a short revue sketch Pinter wrote, two old ladies talk while they eat their soup and wait for a bus. Finally as the two-nine-six approaches one lady observes "It don't look like an all-night bus in daylight, do it?" (127). Her comment describes the way in which we respond to the everyday language of Pinter's characters. For it is only when one finds himself waiting with Rose in a room surrounded by darkness that the most ordinary words take on the aura of imminent peril.

Pinter has reminisced about his youth in Hackney and recalled that being Jewish and unaccompanied was sometimes a dangerous combination. He particularly remembers walks down dark alleys with hooligans clutching broken milk bottles in the shadows. Pinter usually got through on wit, saying, for example,

> "Are you all right?"
> "Yes, I'm all right."
> "Well, that's all right then, isn't it?" [6]

If one may say so, without begging the question, this is pure Pinter dialogue emerging from an atmosphere oppressed by the sullen threat of violence.

The language of *The Room* and the other plays discussed in this chapter is the standard speech of the working classes, a patois informed by the daily fare of sex and violence in *News of the World* and the "telly." Why then does Pinter's conventional transference of this speech to dirty little people in grubby little rooms seem so unconventional? What strikes us as strange in Pinter is often due to the failure of our memory. If, for example, we find ourselves overhearing a conversation on a subway, we expect that there will be numerous gaps or pauses, many sentences left hanging. Events may be described which we can only grasp in part and we find ourselves, almost apart from our will, trying to guess at motives and backgrounds. We do not assume that the characters have no motives, no backgrounds out of which they emerge, or have no good reason for being what they are —we simply are not told these things. If one were to transfer such conversations to the stage that which we take for granted would suddenly seem strange. Such a playwright would hardly seem a realist until we chanced to recall that our everyday existence is charged with just such mystery. The concession we might then be willing to make to Pinter's deployment of language might also be extended to admit in Rose something of our own effort to make an accommodation with the dark and in Riley something resembling the shadow which haunts all civilized men.

The Birthday Party (1957), Pinter's second play, makes "the room" a bit larger, increases the number of characters in that room, and multiplies the complexity of their relationships; but it is also a play about a person who does not want to leave his room. (Like *The Room, The Birthday Party* seems to have had its genesis in an experience which Pinter had on tour when he stayed in a boarding house.) *The Birthday Party* has had a curious history. It opened to nearly unanimous denunciation with only Harold Hobson of the *Sunday Times* praising it. (One performance played to only six people in the audience.) Since then *The Birthday Party* has been reproduced widely in both England and the United States and in 1968 was successfully transferred to the screen. The central figure in *The Birthday Party* is Stanley Webber, a man in his late thirties who resides at a boarding house on the coast. Like Rose, he clings to the security of that house and refuses to go out. But the world cannot be shut out forever and *The Birthday Party* is the story of the destruction of Stanley's security by that external world. Again Pinter does not reveal the exact nature of the threat against Stanley, the strange power the intruders from that world seem to have over him, or the background out of which Stanley has come and which might help explain the circumstances of *The Birthday Party*. In a program note written for a tandem presentation of *The Dumb Waiter* and *The Room* Pinter observed

A character on the stage who can present no convincing argument or information as to his past experience, his present behaviour or his aspirations, nor give a comprehensive analysis of his motives, is as legitimate and as worthy of attention as one who, alarmingly, can do all these things.

The word *alarmingly* suggests that Pinter concludes that the most important details, the vital data are never known, or if known, never fully revealed.

The initial scene of *The Birthday Party* introduces Meg and Petey, the sixty-year-old proprietors of the boarding house. Their conversation overtly revolves around the staples of breakfast, corn flakes and the news. However, it is clear that Meg has her mind on Stanley, their boarder, who is still asleep upstairs. Scattered throughout her mundane conversation with Petey are numerous references to Stanley. She says, for example, that she wished she had a little boy, that she wished Stanley would take her for a walk some day, and finally she expresses concern for the condition of his socks. The bits and pieces are widely scattered but they accumulate over the course of the three acts to show Meg's need to mother Stanley. In the course of this casual conversation Petey also announces that two strangers are interested in staying at the boarding house. Thus, with an economy of characterization and dialogue, Pinter has been able to introduce the warring elements of the drama. We now know that there is a protective circle of warmth and maternal affection around Stanley, but there are also outsiders who are about to penetrate that circle.

It is also clear when Stanley comes to breakfast that Meg may have something more than a maternal interest in Stanley. After she has wrestled him out of bed, she defends herself as a good wife. When Stanley uses the word *succulent* to describe the fried bread, she takes offense, thinking it a sexual reference. In mock anger Stanley calls her a "succulent old washing bag" and she asks

> [*shyly*]: Am I really succulent?
> STANLEY   Oh, you are. I'd rather have you than a cold in the nose any day.
> MEG   You're just saying that.
> STANLEY   [*violently*]: Look, why don't you get this place cleared up! It's a pigsty. And another thing, what about my room? It needs sweeping. It needs papering. I need a new room!
> MEG   [*sensual, stroking his arm*]: Oh, Stan, that's a lovely room. I've had some lovely afternoons in that room. (19)

Again through an economy of dialogue and innuendo, Pinter is able to introduce a mixed bag of maternal need, of sexual attraction, and of suppressed violence.

When Meg drops the information that two strangers are coming to see about a room, Stanley's reaction is seemingly exaggerated. He asks a number of questions about the strangers and appears agitated that they are coming. Perhaps because his isolation is threatened Stanley then begins to talk about a job he has been offered to play the piano in a Berlin night club. As he reminisces about his career he recalls a concert he once gave. Though he played well, the critics "carved me up." No one showed up for subsequent concerts and he has since gone into retirement. Stanley suspects there is a conspiracy against his career. Though Meg is quite willing to give him the adulation he needs, Stanley cannot erase the debacle from his memory. With the notion of a conspiracy in the back of his mind he turns on Meg and begins playing on her fears, the same kind of fears that Rose confessed. "They" are coming, he says. "They" are coming in a van and have a wheelbarrow in that van and are going to cart someone away. Although the threat is implicitly against Meg, Stanley ironically adumbrates his own end.

When Lulu, the only other guest in the house, enters, Stanley pumps her with questions to learn if she knows anything about the strangers and he even suggests to her that they run away together. When she asks where they would go, he confesses he has no plan; he merely wants to get away, to escape. Together the three characters that have been introduced, Meg, Petey, and Lulu, form a protective barrier around Stanley. They help and console him but they cannot save nor protect him.

The battle lines, thus, are drawn. Stanley and his ineffective defenders will try to keep the invaders out. The "invaders" take form with the entry of Goldberg and McCann. Goldberg is the brains of the duo, McCann the muscle. Goldberg is known by various names—Nat, Simey, Benny— and his son was named Emanuel but also called Manny and Timmy. Goldberg is always full of advice, reminiscences, anecdotes. "The secret," he says, "is breathing. Take my tip. It's a well-known fact. Breathe in, breathe out, take a chance, let yourself go, what can you lose? Look at me. When I was an apprentice yet, McCann, every second Friday of the month my Uncle Barney used to take me to the seaside, regular as clockwork . . ." (29). And on he rambles. One critic has noted how Goldberg explains the secret of relaxation but does not relax himself. His phrases are salted with harsh *c*, *ch*, and *k* sounds which belie his gentle demeanor.[7]

McCann is clearly nervous about the "job" they are to do. He begins to ask questions and is cautioned that some things are not for him to know. When McCann persists, Goldberg draws himself up and in a pontifical tone declares,

GOLDBERG   The main issue is a singular issue and quite distinct from your previous work. Certain elements, however, might well approximate in points of procedure to some of your other activities. All is dependent on the attitude of our subject. At all events, McCann, I can assure you that the assignment will be carried out and the mission accomplished with no excessive aggravation to you or myself. Satisfied?

MCCANN   Sure. Thank you, Nat. (32)

Goldberg's speech is a parody of "officialese." He is saying next to nothing, but he says nothing well and McCann is sufficiently impressed to stop asking questions.

Meg gives Goldberg and McCann a room and invites them to a party that evening, a birthday party for Stanley. Stanley claims that it is not his birthday; but Meg insists and presents him with a gift, a child's drum. The first act concludes with Stanley circling Meg and beating the drum. At first the rhythm is regular but soon becomes erratic and uncontrolled. Stanley looms over Meg and beats the drum as though possessed by some demon. The "concert artist" has been reduced to a savage and primitive performer tapping crude cadenzas. There seems no explanation for his behavior other than that the threat which the outsiders represent to his security has thrown him back on rather primitive affects.

One of the ways in which Pinter permits silence to work upon our consciousness is to have the characters engage in seemingly insignificant but compulsively repetitive activities. At first these acts may seem slightly strange or slightly humorous; but as they continue, they become forms of expression for emotions too profound to utter. Stanley's beating of the drum ends the first act, and the second act begins with McCann slowly and mechanically tearing a newspaper into equal strips. Both characters are channeling and expressing their fears and agressions. Davies' repetitious pounding of his fist into his hand in *The Caretaker* is equally revealing of anxieties and hostilities that are more deeply imbedded than his language can fathom. In his *Psychopathology of Everyday Life*, Freud systematically explores precisely such *lapsus linguae* and chance actions that are the external manifestations of inner attitudes. The tension which seems to crackle in the atmosphere of Pinter's plays usually derives from the ways in which these repressed emotions resist being denied their expression.

When Stanley confronts the two intruders, he says he has a feeling that he has met them before. He questions them and asks if they have ever been near Maidenhead where Fuller's teashop, Boots Library, and High Street are located. McCann says they have not (42). But later Goldberg muses, "That's the sort of man I am. Not size but quality. A little

Austin, tea in Fullers, a library book from Boots, and I'm satisfied" (59). The systematic undercutting of the fact is characteristic not only of *The Birthday Party* but of the other works in the Pinter corpus. It is not that the characters are lying (though we do not know that they are not lying); it is simply that we can only see the truth over their shoulders. In an essay "Writing for the Theatre" Pinter observed,

There are at least twenty-four possible aspects of any single statement, depending on where you're standing at the time or on what the weather's like. A categorical statement, I find, will never stay where it is and be finite. It will immediately be subject to modification by the other twenty-three possibilities of it. No statement I make, therefore, should be interpreted as final and definitive.[8]

As the separate testimonies to the "truth" accumulate in Pinter's plays, the "truth" becomes even more uncertain and the "facts" of the matter begin to call each other into question.

Stanley's conversation with McCann and Goldberg does not set his anxiety to rest. His anxiety steadily asserts itself as his identity and way of life seem called into question.

STANLEY You know what? To look at me, I bet you wouldn't think I'd led such a quiet life. The lines on my face, eh? It's the drink. Been drinking a bit down here. But what I mean is . . . you know how it is . . . away from your own . . . all wrong, of course . . . I'll be all right when I get back . . . but what I mean is, the way some people look at me you'd think I was a different person. I suppose I have changed, but I'm still the same man that I always was. I mean, you wouldn't think, to look at me, really . . . I mean, not really, that I was the sort of bloke to—to cause any trouble, would you? [*McCann looks at him*] Do you know what I mean?
MCCANN No. [*As Stanley picks up a strip of paper*] Mind that. (43)

McCann cuts him off sharply and brutally. Stanley seems to be cracking and desperately asks McCann why he is there and how much he knows. McCann feigns innocence, but

Stanley, perceiving danger in their contact, is already on the run.

Stanley has received no answer to his questions; thus McCann and Goldberg begin to ask their questions. The innocent beginning is soon transformed into a savage interrogation.

GOLDBERG   Why are you wasting everybody's time, Webber? Why are you getting in everybody's way?
STANLEY   Me? What are you—
GOLDBERG   I'm telling you, Webber. You're a washout. Why are you getting on everybody's wick? Why are you driving that old lady off her conk?
MCCANN   He likes to do it!
GOLDBERG   Why do you behave so badly, Webber? Why do you force that old man out to play chess?
STANLEY   Me?
GOLDBERG   Why do you treat that young lady like a leper? She's not the leper, Webber!
STANLEY   What the—
GOLDBERG   What did you wear last week, Webber? Where do you keep your suits?
MCCANN   Why did you leave the organization?
GOLDBERG   What would your old mum say, Webber?
MCCANN   Why did you betray us?
GOLDBERG   You hurt me, Webber. You're playing a dirty game.
MCCANN   That's a Black and Tan fact.
GOLDBERG   Who does he think he is?
MCCANN   Who do you think you are? (50, 51)

The question "Who do you think you are?" hangs in the air. Stanley's whole identity is called in doubt by their dialectic. Even his name is stripped from him as a token of his lost identity.

GOLDBERG   Webber! Why did you change your name?
STANLEY   I forgot the other one.
GOLDBERG   What's your name now?
STANLEY   Joe Soap.
GOLDBERG   You stink of sin. . . .
You're dead. You can't live, you can't think, you can't love. You're dead. You're a plague gone bad. There's no juice in you. You're nothing but an odour! (53, 55)

The interrogation of Stanley has all the qualities of a coordinated ritual. Although the nature of the indictment is never clear, it is apparent that Stanley is guilty or thinks he is guilty. His guilt is like that which Kafka describes in *The Trial*.

> "But I am not guilty," said K. "it's a mistake. And, if it comes to that, how can any man be called guilty? We are all simply men here, one is as much as the other."
> "That's true," said the priest, "but that's how all guilty men talk."

Guilt is presumed independent of any acts. Stanley is weighed and found wanting and the final docility with which he accepts the verdict is indicative of his acceptance of the guilt. Earlier that day Stanley had warned Meg that someone was coming to get her and cart her away. Meg's response suggested not only that she was frightened by this unspecified threat but that she too might be implicated in some secret guilt. Their self-consciousness of guilt-ridden involvement seems to lie just below the surface and needs only the press of external events to trigger its release.

The interrogation and the violence it unleashes is interrupted by the entry of Meg who wants to begin the birthday party. The party is the center of the play, the nexus of the two circles around Stanley, one protective, one destructive. The party begins and the lights are turned off. A flashlight is shined on Stanley, "the birthday boy," while maudlin speeches in his honor are delivered. Stanley has only moved from one spotlight to another, but ironically his friends do not perceive the danger he is in. The climax of the party is a game of "blind man's buff" in which Stanley becomes the victim. While Stanley is blindfolded, McCann shatters his glasses and Stanley finds himself pushed into darkness and further isolated like Rose at the conclusion of *The Room*. The second act ends when Stanley, put upon by the visitors and terrified by recent disclosures, tries to strangle Meg and rape Lulu. At the end of act 1, he had been pushed back upon his deepest and most primitive emotions and act 2 concludes with the total dissolution of his personality and his reversion into primitivism.

The last act takes place the following morning. Stanley's friends have never quite understood what went on the night before, and they are waiting for an explanation. A large car sits outside and Meg wonders vaguely whether there is a wheelbarrow in it. Apparently she recalls the threat to her own person some twenty-four hours earlier. When Stanley finally enters, he is radically transformed. His unkempt appearance of the day before has yielded to striped trousers, black jacket, white collar, and a bowler in one hand and broken glasses in the other. He is taciturn, almost somnambulant, totally shattered. Goldberg and McCann promise to take care of his every need, and they commence a litany that runs for minutes and concludes with

GOLDBERG   We'll make a man of you.
MCCANN   And a woman.
GOLDBERG   You'll be re-orientated.
MCCANN   You'll be rich.
GOLDBERG   You'll be adjusted.
MCCANN   You'll be our pride and joy.
GOLDBERG   You'll be a mensch.
MCCANN   You'll be a success.
GOLDBERG   You'll be integrated.
MCCANN   You'll give orders.
GOLDBERG   You'll make decisions.
MCCANN   You'll be a magnate.
GOLDBERG   A statesman.
MCCANN   You'll own yachts.
GOLDBERG   Animals.
MCCANN   Animals. (88)

The litany is meaningless and meaningful at the same time. Goldberg and McCann are the spinners of a web of words which Stanley cannot escape. His only reply to their promises is an anguished cry. In his dehumanized state he has passed beyond the recourse of language to silence.

Goldberg and McCann remove Stanley, saying that an unidentified Monty will take care of him. When Petey protests on behalf of Stanley's friends, he is told that maybe

Monty would like to see him too. The anonymous threat is enough to silence Petey. Meg wanders in and dreamily recollects how she was the belle of the ball at the party the night before. "I know I was," she says as Stanley is drawn from the room, not to life but to death. For Meg and her outer circle the party was a celebration, a drunken spree. For those of the inner circle it was the systematic tightening of a noose. For Stanley it was a *Totentanz* whereby he danced from the internal to the external *agon.*

Again the temptation is to allegorize Pinter. For example, the number of references to Ireland [9] suggest that Stanley like Johnny Boyle in O'Casey's *Juno and the Paycock* may have betrayed the I.R.A. and now is receiving his just retribution. A more subtle allegory takes its cue from Stanley's apparent vocation. Hoefer argues that Stanley is the artist who must "resist the strait jacket of clichés which society would force on him." [10] But we have only Stanley's word that he is an artist of concert caliber; anyone can beat a drum and Stanley does not even do that well. In Hoefer's allegory McCann and Goldberg are the representatives of the bourgeois world. Goldberg is full of homey maxims and platitudes.

> All my life I've said the same. Play up, play up, and play the game. Honour thy father and thy mother. All along the line. Follow the line, the line, McCann, and you can't go wrong. What do you think, I'm a self-made man? No! I sat where I was told to sit. I kept my eye on the ball. School? Don't talk to me about school. Top in all subjects. And for why? Because I'm telling you, I'm telling you, follow my line? Follow my mental? Learn by heart. Never write down a thing. No. And don't go too near the water. And you'll find—that what I say is true. Because I believe that the world . . . [*vacant*] . . . Because I believe that the world . . . [*desperate*] . . . *Because I believe that the world . . . [lost].* . . . (80)

He is a kind of desperate Polonius offering advice to his inferiors. Play the game, he says. In his attention to the world alone, he seems to merge the biblical injunction to honor one's parents with the modern success ethic. He is everybody's Jewish grandfather, but he is also, perhaps, a rattled professional killer who wants to reassure McCann who is a more recent entrant into the game. Goldberg is called Nat and like Nathan the prophet who was charged by God to rebuke David for straying from the path of righteousness, Nat brings the word of reprimand from the omniscient organization to an erring Stanley.[11]

Or one can see in Goldberg the Jewish tradition of family, authority, and property being supported by the Irish Catholic McCann. When Goldberg seems run down, he asks McCann to breathe into him and revitalize him (82). McCann's breath is the spirit (*esprit, spiritus*) which gives life to Jewish tradition. Stanley then is the Protestant individual crushed between the implacable forces of history. Or one can see the two as ministers of death who, like Riley of *The Room*, have come to call Stanley to his real home. Or the two represent "the hostile, unknowable power that takes the place of God in the avant-garde drama's philosophical view of the human condition."[12] Still another allegorical option arises from the frequent homosexual allusions. Men are struggling for men in a strange love-hate atmosphere; McCann periodically "blows" Goldberg, and Stanley is to be turned into a man-woman (88). Stanley, the allegorist would have it, has fled some sort of homosexual brotherhood and his continued estrangement is a threat to the psychological, or before recent parliamentary reform, legal security of the group.

Finally none of these explanations is satisfying. We never know for certain that Goldberg and McCann are killers; perhaps they are from an asylum and are trying to return a patient. We never know who Stanley is; it is likely that he is using an alias and perhaps even his musical career is part of his cover identity. *The Birthday Party* resists all allegory. Pinter has left too many loopholes for the one-to-one identification which allegory demands. To allegorize Pinter one must also assume the author to have a preconceived plan for the play. In the Tynan interview on BBC, Pinter expressly declared that he did not.[13] Rather he explained, the idea grew out of the concrete situation. The characters, in effect, make the idea of the play and not the reverse. In an interview at the time of the filming of *The Birthday Party* Pinter further disclaimed any allegorical intentions.

I *don't* know who Goldberg and McCann are, apart from being Goldberg and McCann. Monty is a fact. All we know about Stanley's past is what he says about it, and that can't be the whole truth. He has lived and has a past, but what he says is all he can say of it. Not every fact is an accurate assessment of what has taken place, but some facts have to be faced. What Stanley says about his concert is based on fact, and, for my money, Goldberg and McCann have come down to get Stanley.

The Birthday Party, then, is not a tissue of systematic signification, the requirement of allegory, but an elaboration, an exfoliation of existential givens.

Even though Stanley may not consider himself legally guilty of anything, he seems to accept the fact that retribution cannot be avoided. He seems to understand the imminence of this retribution when he learns that the strangers have finally arrived. His helplessness in the face of the intruders who have breeched his haven conveys not so much his physical but his psychological enervation. He cannot save himself and he cannot be saved by others. Petey and Lulu were undoubtedly always ineffectual and Meg dotters along oblivious to the *Walpurgis Nacht* that transpired in her parlor. She dreams of being the belle of the ball escorted by her son-lover Stanley.

The mysterious authority of Goldberg and McCann over Stanley should not be a surprise to those who have stood the watch with K. before the castle, to those who have sat and waited by the roadside with Vladimir and Estragon for someone who, apparently, is not coming, or to those who break off their conversations to pay obeisance to the telephone which rings in the other room. Nor can the reduction of Stanley be unaccountable to those who have understood the transformation of Gregor Samsa into a cockroach, or the underground man into a mouse, or have seen Prufrock pinned to the wall. For, like Oedipus, we all seem to carry within us the sense of secret guilt and a suspicion that sooner or later someone will come around to collect on debts outstanding.

The playing with names and labels in *The Birthday Party* seems again to underline the nameless character of the threat which confronts Stanley. One may wish to allegorize that threat, to find its referents and classify them. But to put a label on someone else's guilt, to name the retribution makes it possible for the observer to avoid the radical implications of the play. Someone is coming in a van today to cart you away—to cart *you* away! When the knock on the door finally comes, you will not run but will welcome it with relief, for the wait has been tedious and you would rather pay what you owe and embrace your debtors.

In *The Birthday Party* Goldberg and McCann seem the omnipotent dealers of death. They have the dark gods who pull the strings on their side. But in *The Dumb Waiter* (1957) the professional killers or "debt collectors" are shown to be as vulnerable as Stanley was. They are capable of the same spoken and unspoken fears, the same anxieties, the same conviction of guilt. Apparently the unnamed terrors which afflict Stanley are common to others. That it is the killers who now are threatened may be ironic, but their security can no more be assumed than any other man's.

Two men, Gus and Ben, are on assignment and wait for the specific details in a basement room. Life for the two is a "slow dance on the killing ground." They are bored; they are surrounded by silence; they wait. Ben reads the paper while Gus fidgets. Amid the mundane stories which Ben quotes from the newspaper Gus interjects, "I hope it won't be a long job, this one." There is no answer from Ben who reads another story. "What time is he getting in touch?" There is no rise from Ben and Gus takes another tack.

GUS [*moves to the foot of Ben's bed*]   Well, I was going to ask you something.
BEN   What?
GUS   Have you noticed the time that tank takes to fill?
BEN   What tank?

GUS   In the lavatory.
BEN   No. Does it?
GUS   Terrible.
BEN   Well, what about it?
GUS   What do you think's the matter with it?
BEN   Nothing.
GUS   Nothing?
BEN   It's got a deficient ballcock, that's all.
GUS   A deficient what?
BEN   Ballcock.
GUS   No? Really?
BEN   That's what I should say.
GUS   Go on! That didn't occur to me. (88, 89)

Pinter possesses a heightened sense for the dramatic which one sometimes also finds in the Hitchcock film. Our attention is focused on the most mundane details even while we know that something more important is afoot. We suspect there is going to be a murder, and we find ourselves worried about a defective ballcock. Gus and Ben fill the air with words about deficient ballcocks because they are unwilling or unable to broach the more important matter at hand. The circumlocutory character of Gus' speech is tantamount to a confession that he cannot say what he really wants to say. He is a professional who feels very unprofessional. As Boulton rightly observed of their halting exchanges, "the language is appropriate to characters whose sense of security extends no further than the length of a few words." [14]

Ben attempts to deal with Gus's insecurity.

BEN   You know what your trouble is?
GUS   What?
BEN   You haven't got any interests.
GUS   I've got interests.
BEN   What? Tell me one of your interests.
       [pause]
GUS   I've got interests.
BEN   Look at me. What have I got?
GUS   I don't know. What?
BEN   I've got my woodwork. I've got my model boats. Have
       you ever seen me idle? I'm never idle. I know how to

>   occupy my time, to its best advantage. Then when a
>   call comes. I'm ready.
> GUS   Don't you ever get a bit fed up?
> BEN   Fed up? What with?
>   [*silence*] (90)

Their conversation, having pushed Gus to the brink of his
personal abyss, is resolved in silence. Ben cannot confront
the abyss either but he keeps his hands busy. He is perfectly
adjusted. Idle hands are the devil's playthings, Ben would
likely argue. But Gus does not have recourse to hobbies; he is
a malcontent; he has recourse only to silence.

Because Gus is discomfited he thinks on the origin of his
malaise, the mysterious head of the organization which employs them. "He doesn't seem to bother much about our
comfort these days." Later, "when's he going to get in
touch?" (91, 94). Ben is preoccupied with his newspaper,
but Gus is raising questions about the impersonal authority
that guides their destiny. Suddenly, mysteriously, an envelope containing twelve matches is slid beneath the door.
There is no message on the envelope, and Gus hurries into
the hall to catch the visitor. He returns.

> GUS   No one. [*He replaces the revolver*]
> BEN   What did you see?
> GUS   Nothing.
> BEN   They must have been pretty quick. (96)

Ben ascribes the mystery to someone fleet of foot but to Gus
the incident only increases his inexplicable sense of forebod-
ing, his awareness that the answers to his questions are not
forthcoming.

The conversation which passes between the two is a circle
of advances and retreats. Gus occasionally has the determina-
tion to raise questions about what they are doing there and
what they will be expected to do. But then, just as quickly,
Pinter shunts the conversation off on a sidetrack. Gus and
Ben argue at some length, for example, over whether or not
one should say "light the kettle" or "light the gas." Finally
Ben resolves the quarrel by grabbing Gus by the throat and
screaming "THE KETTLE, YOU FOOL!" (98). More

than an argument in semantics over an Englishman's tea is at stake. Gus questions and Ben resolves the question by the strength of his hands. Idle hands are. . . .

But Gus cannot give up so easily. "I thought perhaps you —I mean—have you got any idea who it's going to be tonight?" he stumbles. He wonders about the mysterious Wilson who may or may not be coming to give them details of their assignment.

> You go to this address, there's a key there, there's a teapot, there's never a soul in sight—[*He pauses*] Eh, nobody ever hears a thing, have you ever thought of that? We never get any complaints, do we, too much noise or anything like that? You never see a soul, do you—except the bloke who comes. You ever noticed that? I wonder if the walls are soundproof. [*He touches the wall above his bed*] Can't tell. All you do is wait, eh? Half the time he doesn't even bother to put in an appearance, Wilson.
> BEN   Why should he? He's a busy man. (101)

When Gus wonders who cleans up after they have gone, Ben tells him that they are only one branch of a large organization and that "they got departments for everything." (103)

In the midst of this chilling discussion about murder and the organization, a dumbwaiter clatters to their level and frightens them by its abrupt appearance. In the dumbwaiter there is a note requesting two braised steaks and chips, two sago puddings, and two teas without sugar. While they regard the note, the dumbwaiter clatters up and Gus cries, "Give us a chance! They're in a hurry, aren't they?" Gus thinks the dumbwaiter intrusion adds to the mystery; but Ben has a ready explanation: the house must have been a restaurant and their basement room is the former kitchen. Gus wants to know who runs the restaurant now and is left only with the obvious conclusion that they have inherited the obligation.

The dumbwaiter returns making more and more demands which seem ridiculous to those who are in the shabby basement but may well make perfect sense to those above who think themselves in a restaurant. Gus and Ben thus find themselves enjoined to conjure soup of the day, liver and onions, jam tart, Macaroni Pastitsio, Ormitha Macarounada

out of the sack lunches they have brought. In their desperation to please those upstairs, in their eagerness to avoid
suspicion, they curiously look very much like Laurel and
Hardy on assignment in the kitchen. They exercise their
confusions and inadequacies like other Music Hall comics
who, were we to take them seriously, become almost unbear-
ably poignant and darkly absurd. As Baudelaire reminds us,
"There are no tears and there is no laughter in Paradise, for
they, both of them, are the children of sorrow."

The tension of fulfilling the unreasonable demands seems
to get to Gus first, and he remembers why they are in the
small room in the first place.

> Why doesn't he get in touch? I feel like I've been here
> years. [*He takes his revolver out of its holster to check
> the ammunition*] We've never let him down though,
> have we? We've never let him down. I was thinking only
> the other day, Ben. We're reliable, aren't we? (109)

Finally Gus despairs and tries to tell those upstairs that "we
can't do it, we haven't got it" (110). He grabs the speaking
tube and defiantly yells "The larder's bare!" (111). But Ben
grabs the tube and speaks deferentially to those upstairs and
explains that they have run out of food. He seems the only
one in control of himself; he seems the only one capable of
communication with those outside the room. The voice in
the tube complains to Ben that the food they sent up was
stale, melted, or sour and that they should now send up some
tea. Furthermore, the voice says they should "light the kettle," siding with Ben's position in the semantic confusion.
Gus's isolation is thus intensified. All of the anxieties he has,
all of the hostility he feels toward those in authority he
projects on those presently upstairs. "They do all right," he
says, "don't worry about that. You don't think they're just
going to sit there and wait for stuff to come up from down
here, do you? That'll get them nowhere" (114). In his state
of utter dependency Gus projects independence on those up
there who will manage quite well, thank you, with or without his puny labors. It is all "past a joke, in my opinion," he
concludes (114).

Ben finally notes that time is getting on. The consumma-

tion of their assignment must be close. He runs through their
final instructions, a scene which hauntingly echoes the litany
of Goldberg and McCann with Stanley. The murder has
been well planned; all that is needed is a victim. But in the
course of the litany Gus realizes,

> You've missed something out.
>
> BEN   I know. What?
> GUS   I haven't taken my gun out, according to you.
> BEN   You take your gun out—
> GUS   After I've closed the door.
> BEN   After you've closed the door.
> GUS   You've never missed that out before, you know that?
> BEN   When he sees you behind him—
> GUS   Me behind him—
> BEN   And me in front of him—
> GUS   And you in front of him—
> BEN   He'll feel uncertain—
> GUS   Uneasy.
> BEN   He won't know what to do.
> GUS   So what will he do?
> BEN   He'll look at me and he'll look at you.
> GUS   We won't say a word.
> BEN   We'll look at him.
> GUS   He won't say a word.
> BEN   He'll look at us.
> GUS   And we'll look at him.
> BEN   Nobody says a word. (115, 116)

The rehearsal for the killing even tells us what the victim
will look like and how silence will reign in that moment of
confrontation.

As they wait those last moments Gus cannot stop from
questioning the bizzare chain of events, the relationship of
their assignment here below with the disembodied com-
mands which issue from above.

> GUS   [thickly]: Who is it upstairs?
> BEN   [nervously]: What's one thing to do with another?
> GUS   Who is it, though?
> BEN   What's one thing to do with another? (117)

Ben treats each phenomenon as discrete and unrelated, but
Gus senses a tightening web of circumstances with him at

the center. The rhetoric of irony is to say one thing and mean another; the irony of existence is to be one thing and mean another. It is Gus who has been raising the question of meaning from the beginning while Ben has been unable to see what one thing has to do with another. But now Gus like Stanley can only struggle to avoid the judgment which he senses is being levied against him. His life has had a certain meaning to him, but someone else has examined the evidence and reached a different conclusion. Gus can only protest,

> [*passionately, advancing*] What's he doing it for? We've been through our tests, haven't we? We got right through our tests, years ago, didn't we? We took them together, don't you remember, didn't we? We've proved ourselves before now, haven't we? We've always done our job. What's he doing all this for? What's the idea? What's he playing these games for? (118)

At that moment the dumbwaiter rattles down and in desperation Gus screams in the tube: "WE'VE GOT NOTHING LEFT! NOTHING! DO YOU UNDERSTAND?" (118)

Gus sits in silence and Ben reads the paper, commenting here and there on stories but never making the facts of those stories clear to Gus. Finally Gus wanders out of the room in search of water. While he is gone a message comes through the tube that Ben is to ready himself to kill the victim who has now arrived and will shortly present himself at the door. Gus opens the door and, stripped of his coat and tie and gun, stares at his executioner in silence.

The Dumb Waiter has a number of motifs in common with *The Room* and *The Birthday Party*. But most importantly, in all three someone sits anxiously within a room and regards each intrusion into that room as the externalization of a threat long felt but unsusceptible to complete articulation. For this reason the sundry silences of the three plays are perhaps more important to our understanding of those characters than whatever they may say overtly. For example, a dumb waiter is a silent waiter; Gus is a silent waiter; he waits for that final silence wherein his destiny will manifest itself. But on the other hand, Ben is a dumb waiter. It is Gus who questions everything and because of his constant interrogation, he becomes a threat to the hierarchy and must be removed. In thinking too long on the victims, Gus makes himself eligible to become a victim.

It is as tempting to allegorize *The Dumb Waiter* as well as Pinter's other plays. For example, the mysterious "he," the hierarchical power upstairs could be identified as a diety. Those who play the God-game like Ben get along, but those who question His ways are rubbed out. The little creatures scurry about on their terrestrial plane and try to guess what the bossman wants of them. His laws are arbitrary and offenders are summarily executed. His interventions are either mystifying or outrageously demanding. Ben and Gus, then, are troubled humanity in the hands of an angry or indifferent God. When Gus says the larder's bare and that they have no more to give, he means that men are played out, drained of their will to continue a game they did not begin and cannot conclude.

But it is not necessary to allegorize *The Dumb Waiter* to feel the compelling power of Pinter's dramatization of men ignorant of their assignment. It is not necessary to identify the mysterious voice with the Deity to understand man's suspicion that there is a power that is not so much malevolent as detached and unconcerned about those dancing on the killing ground beneath. There seem finally two ways of responding to the absence of answers to a man's questions. He may continue his frustration by asking himself additional questions until he has pushed himself to the abyss. Or he can simply continue to play the game and hope he does not stumble along the way. Gus and Ben personify this central dilemma.

GUS   He might not come. He might just send a message. He
       doesn't always come.
BEN   Well, you'll have to do without it, won't you? (100)

The limitation of set in *The Dumb Waiter* and the other plays of "the room" metaphor obviously goes beyond the need to pare costs, beyond any desire to heed the so-called classical unities. It is rather a strategy to compress a situation, to focus on its central tension as a means of making manifest the Angst-ridden isolation of the characters in those rooms. What one may wish to make of those characters in those situations becomes the problem. Those who avoid allegory have Pinter's blessing.

I've never started a play from any kind of abstract idea or theory and never envisaged my own characters as messengers of death, doom, heaven or the milky way or, in other words, as allegorical representations of any particular force, whatever that may mean. When a character cannot be comfortably defined or understood in terms of the familiar, the tendency is to perch him on a symbolic shelf, out of harm's way. Once there, he can be talked about but need not be lived with.[15]

But allegory is not the only option. Pinter is right to insist on the concrete identity of his characters. We are all creatures within a set of givens, our *Dasein*. But we are also within a context which is trans-personal and wherein we touch on destinies not our own. We are here, but we also wander through the trackless spaces of the collective imagination. Only after we have moved beyond the concrete, can we return to it and savor the rough edges of its particularity. We do not have to say that Riley is "Death" to confess that we wait in silence for some Riley to knock upon our door. We do not have to answer to the name of Rose, or Stanley, or Gus to confess that we have been living in their rooms for some time.

2

The Poverty of Self
A Slight Ache, The Lover

Copeau's familiar observation that "the theatre and reality meet only to destroy each other" needs modification when dealing with Pinter. He does not trade realism for allegory or symbolism. Rather, he undermines what we take to be reality with what he takes to be reality. Pinter's theatre is consequently given to psychological realism rather than to social realism. His preoccupation is with the isolated individual and not the machinations of mace or mitre or suffering masses. But he is, paradoxically, more the realist than the realists. He cuts his "slice of life" thinner and thereby makes it more nearly translucent. Though he may portray a mad society, the basic commitment of the realist is to reason—the reasoned analysis, the reasoned solution. Pinter has no necessary obligation to reason, for his province is the psyche where there are things unaccountable to ratiocinative man. For example, precisely because of his ear for the cadences of English speech Pinter can sustain the illusion of mundane conversation at the same time he reveals the emptiness and "baseless fabric" of those who use that language. Or, another example, the preoccupation of characters with the results of football matches or flies caught in marmalade seems disarmingly innocent. At the same time the unspoken fears, doubts, hopes of these characters hover behind the overtly realistic scenes and render their claims for credibility inconclusive.

In plays like *The Blacks* and *The Balcony* Jean Genet explores the question which Pirandello raised in *Six Characters in Search of an Author* and *Henry IV* and which Pinter continues in *A Slight Ache*—who is the real person? Genet and Pirandello suggest that human personality is a transient fiction, a cluster of illusions which hides the nothingness at the center. Previously in Pinter one never discovered what any character's personality really was. The characters were all too frightened to undertake any probing self-analysis. In *A Slight Ache* (1959) we see at last characters who discover the truth of their identities.

In *Waiting for Godot* Estragon declares, "We are happy. (*silence*) What do we do now, now that we are happy?" *A Slight Ache* abandons the grubby little characters in dingy rooms for a look at the other half, the affluent set who have the security of wealth, estate, and position. Now that they are happy, now that they are secure what are they to do? What lies at the center of "the beautiful people"? Where is the threat to those whose position is unassailable? *A Slight Ache* makes it impossible for us to misunderstand the plays of "the room" metaphor. The obvious sources of danger have been removed but the threat remains. The threat, we finally conclude, is not without but within.

Edward and Flora are observed at the breakfast table of their country home. Beyond them we can see an ordered garden. The two are mildly arguing over the flowers in their garden, whether the shrub outside the toolshed is japonica or convolvulus. Edward is wrong and concludes,

> I don't see why I should be expected to distinguish between these plants. It's not my job.
> FLORA   You know perfectly well what grows in your garden.
> EDWARD   Quite the contrary. It is clear that I don't. (10)

In some sense the problem Edward faces throughout the play is to discover what grows in his garden, what vegetates closest to home.

While they sit idly chatting, Edward traps a wasp in the marmalade and seems to enjoy his superiority over the hapless creature. Flora concludes, "What a horrible death," but Edward disagrees, rather fancying that particular kind of departure from life. In this nook surrounded by flowers a wasp is dying and Edward fails to perceive that perhaps he too is dying a sweet death while surrounded by the smothering attention of his "Flora." Edward, it seems, has had some problem seeing things lately. He has "a slight ache" in the back of his eyes. Nothing serious. Nothing to worry about. Just a slight ache.

While Flora natters on about the flowers, Edward curses when he perceives a matchseller standing at the foot of the garden. Edward's indignation seems disproportionate to the offense. "Why? What is he doing there?" he angrily repeats. As Gus learned in *The Dumb Waiter*, one who asks questions may learn some disconcerting answers. Edward paces back and forth fuming,

> For two months he's been standing on that spot, do you realize that? Two months. I haven't been able to step outside the back gate. (15)

The matchseller seems to have some talismanic presence for Edward. He cannot approach the matchseller and send him packing as he ought. "Of course he's harmless. How could he be other than harmless," Edward convinces himself (16). When Flora looks at the matchseller down by the garden gate, she sees something else.

> Good Lord, what's that? Is that a bullock let loose? No. It's the matchseller! My goodness, you can see him . . . through the hedge. He looks bigger. Have you been watching him? He looks . . . like a bullock. (17)

When Flora suggests that Edward may be frightened by the matchseller, Edward protests that he is not, but his protest tapers off into a complaint about his eyes; it seems they have a slight ache. But Edward must confront the matchseller.

> It's quite absurd, of course. I really can't tolerate something so . . . absurd, right on my doorstep.

A moment later he concludes,

> He's not a matchseller at all. The bastard isn't a matchseller at all. Curious I never realized that before. He's an imposter. . . . No, there is something very false about that man. I intend to get to the bottom of it. I'll soon

get rid of him. He can go and ply his trade somewhere
else. Instead of standing like a bullock . . . a bullock,
outside my back gate. (19)

Accordingly Edward embarks upon the ironic venture to
exorcise the unwanted demon from his premises. He, the
man hiding from himself, seeks to root the imposter from his
life. He invites the matchseller in so that he can deal with
him as a master deals with a subordinate, as a man deals with
a wasp.

The matchseller enters and stands without expression or
gesture before Edward. Edward is quite courteous, the perfect host. The matchseller is silent and does not make the
slightest response. Edward explains his position of eminence
to the visitor. He writes theological and philosophical essays,
does some exploring, and in general leads a rather interesting
life. The matchseller is silent.

Edward empathizes with the visitor and explains how he
too was once in the less fortunate position of the matchseller. With persistence and drive and a good woman at his
side, however, he triumphed. The matchseller is silent. Edward offers another drink. He examines the matchseller's
soggy wares and looks into his eyes. The matchseller is silent.
Finally, in desperation Edward says,

> Forgive me for saying so, but I had decided that you had
> the comprehension of a bullock. I was mistaken. You
> understand me perfectly well. . . . You may think I was
> alarmed by the look of you. You would be quite mistaken.
> I was not alarmed by the look of you. I did not find you
> at all alarming. No, no. Nothing outside this room has
> ever alarmed me. You disgusted me, quite forcibly, if you
> want to know the truth. (26, 27)

Exhausted he retreats to the garden for a breath of air.

Throughout the course of the interrogation, the matchseller has said nothing but Edward has talked on maniacally.
The scene is reminiscent of Rose's conversations with herself
while Bert sat dumbly at the breakfast table. The more he
talks, the more agonized Edward seems. His conversation is
filled with elliptical pauses, points at which he can go no

further in language. His effort to embellish his image before the decrepit matchseller makes it clear that Edward is very unsure of himself and is trying to cover the fact that he is not what he would appear to be. The unspoken truth about Edward seems to emerge from the silence behind his language, the silence of a man who has nothing important to say, the silence of an empty self.

When Flora questions Edward about the progress of his examination, Edward says they are getting on rather well. The matchseller is a bit reticent although, "It's understandable. I should be the same, perhaps, in his place. Though, of course, I could not possibly find myself in his place" (28). The *peripeteia* of the conclusion underscores the irony of Edward's unintentional insight. He has always been in the place of the matchseller and has only been waiting for the day to arrive when the matchseller made his appearance.

But Flora senses that Edward has failed to produce any concrete results and decides to have a go herself.

> Do you know, I've got a feeling I've seen you before, somewhere. Long before the flood. You were much younger. Yes, I'm really sure of it. Between ourselves, were you ever a poacher? I had an encounter with a poacher once. It was a ghastly rape, the brute. . . . (31)

Flora also seems to be projecting her personal history onto the matchseller. She claims an experience of *deja vu*, a recollection of something familiar in the visitor. She mops his brow, claiming that such is a woman's obligation and she is the only woman on hand. She asks him what he thinks of sex, she fondles him, she decides to give him a bath. Finally she throws her arms around him and says, "I'm going to keep you. I'm going to keep you, you dreadful chap, and call you Barnabas. Isn't it dark Barnabas? Your eyes, your eyes, your great big eyes" (32). Flora, it seems, has also been waiting for "Barnabas" for some time. Now that he has arrived, the personification of her fantasies, she can be both wife and mother to him even as Meg fantasized about Stanley. Barnabas was the only character admitted to Kafka's *Castle* and this second Barnabas has also apparently merited access to the center of the household.[1] In his large, dark eyes, portal to his depths, Flora apparently finds what she has not been able to find in the aching eyes of Edward.

Edward returns and viciously dismisses Flora. He turns to the matchseller.

> Make yourself at home. Strip to your buff. Do as you would in your own house.
> [*pause*]
> Did you say something?
> [*pause*]
> Did you say something?
> [*pause*]
> Anything? (34)

Edward cannot stand the silence which confronts him. The silence is disconcerting to him because it is a silence that throws the burden of conversation back upon him. He cannot support the silence because he has nothing to offer to the abyss. His plea for assistance fails and he natters on about cricket. Edward's perplexity is ironically compounded by the fact that he is the source of that silence. His confusion parallels that of a character in Beckett's *Murphy* who is

spattered with words that went dead as soon as they sounded; each word obliterated before it had time to make sense by the word that came next; so that in the end [he] did not know what had been said.

But once Edward's expectations have broken down, he confesses a sense of *deja vu* comparable to that of Flora. He has seen the matchseller before but on those previous occasions the visitor looked somewhat different.

> In fact every time I have seen you, you have looked quite different to the time before.
> [*pause*]
> Even now you look different. Very different.
> [*pause*]
> Admitted that sometimes I viewed you through dark glasses, yes, and sometimes through light glasses, and on other occasions bare eyed. (37)

It seems that Edward has been confronting similar reminders of his emptiness for some time.

The process by which Pinter takes Edward from a cocky, self-assured author to a snivelling dog that cowers before a man who does not speak is as subtle as it is terrifying. Edward's monologues are in fact dialogues, not between himself and the visitor but between himself and himself. He is engaged in questioning himself, and he finds that the answers are destructive. In the dialectic of examination, he discovers the synthesis, the final term, is emptiness. With a final plea he asks the matchseller, "who are you?" The silence which ensues is the silence which emerges from the poverty of his own condition.

Flora enters calling the name of her beloved Barnabas. She wants to show him her garden, now his garden. As an after-thought she hands Edward the tray of matches as she and the matchseller leave together.

The conclusion of A *Slight Ache*, while shocking, is not surprising. Pinter has prepared the audience for the exchange of roles in his dissection of Edward and Flora. Whether or not the matchseller exists seems immaterial. The audience does not see him for the first half of the play; and the same point might be made, and perhaps better made, if Edward cast his weak eyes on vacancy. It is vacancy that the play explores and the matchseller only serves as an objective correlative for the emotions of Edward and Flora. The image of the "bullock," for example, is indicative. Flora describes the matchseller as a bullock and projects on him the strength and virility which she misses in Edward. Even the name she chooses for him reflects his barnyard animality. Edward, at first convinced of his own strength, nevertheless returns again and again to the word "bullock" as he begins projecting his particular fantasies onto the stranger.

Edward's virility seems to be one of the crucial points of contention among this bizzare *ménage à trois*. The play takes place the longest day of the year, but Edward is bothered by the fecund heat and brilliance of the sun. He reprimands Flora a number of times, especially when she calls him by her pet name "Beddie-Weddie." The obvious sexual reference is offensive to Edward and the reminder of what he ought to be becomes even more acute when Flora calls the matchseller a "bullock." Edward's eye problem may well suggest his inability to see things as they really are, but the condition of his eyes at the end of the play is also a kind of symbolic emasculation like that which afflicted Stanley when his glasses were broken. The slight ache, then, parallels his declining vigor and inability to deal with the world before him. Edward thus sees darkly in the matchseller's blank face the image of his own impotence.

The related theme of the exchange of identity also intrigues Pinter. In his short story "The Examination" (1959), for example, Pinter traces the gradual exchange of roles between master and mastered. The narrator brags of his dominance over Kullus, the person being questioned, and how he has the examination in hand. However, it is in the silences, the pauses between their conversations that the narrator seems forced back upon himself and slowly, because of his weakness, he becomes dominated by Kullus. He explains the transformation,

> the nature of our silences, which formerly were distinct in their opposition: that is, a silence within the frame of our examination, and a silence outside the frame of our examination; seemed to me no longer opposed, indeed were indistinguishable, and were one silence, dictated by Kullus. (91)

In his film script for *The Servant* (1963) Pinter similarly depicts the way in which Barrett, the servant, usurps the leadership of the household. In *The Compartment* (1963) (later known as *The Basement* [1967]), a television play, Pinter explores the process by which Tim Law, who sits comfortably in his warm home, is supplanted by Stott and Jane who enter on a cold, rainy evening. At the conclusion Tim and Jane knock at the door which is answered by Stott who has been sitting in his warm room reading. The cycle of replacement, apparently, will continue.

Other themes which Pinter dramatized in *A Slight Ache* include the psychological stratagems of projection and reaction formation, and the theme of blindness. In his sketch *Request Stop* (1959), for example, a woman waiting in a bus line accuses a man of making improper advances. The man is incapable of replying while she denounces him loudly so that others may hear of the insult to her character. When the bus comes, everyone gets on, but the woman who moves to another line and sidles up to another stranger, ready again to project upon him her unspoken needs. In *A Night Out* (1960), a radio-television play, a young man named Albert attempts to break away from his possessive mother. He ultimately finds himself in a room with a prostitute upon whom he projects all of the hostility which he has been unable to unleash upon his mother. Having undergone a kind of catharsis, he returns home and docilely submits to his mother's obsessive solicitude. Albert manifests that same poverty of character that Edward discovers. He has great intelligence but no moral core and thus is dominated by the possessive mother.

In *The Tea Party* (1964), read by Pinter on the BBC, Disson, a successful manufacturer of bidets, is slowly going blind. The blindness seems proportionate to his growing questions about himself and the security of his position. Finally he succumbs to what appears to be a psychosomatic blindness during a nightmarish tea party, a party which from his dimmed perspective affords only glimpses of distorted masks and seems the prelude to his own dark night of the soul.[2] All of these themes have exercised Pinter's imagination but they converge most successfully in *A Slight Ache*.

In *The Room*, *The Birthday Party*, and *The Dumb Waiter*, the menace seemed a hidden but imminent force outside. In *A Slight Ache*, however, the characters are enabled to see outside and project their sense of menace on the harmless matchseller. When they invite that menace into their home, however, we learn that the danger has always been within and not without. The narrow room has been opened to numerous vistas but the menace remains; the individual still finds himself enclosed within the self.

Other playwrights have attempted to depict a similar generation of hollow men. Ionesco's well-known *The Bald Soprano* is perhaps typical. When Ionesco began to learn English, he discovered the vacuity of the words we use, and, concomitantly, of the people who use them. Thus *The Bald Soprano* is composed largely of the clichés of the language primer. Ionesco has further described the emptiness of those who use the language and the way in which their personalities are so similar that characters like Edward might well exchange identities and never be noticed. This emptiness of the self is best conveyed linguistically by

all that is automatic in the language and behaviour of people; "talking for the sake of talking," talking because there is nothing personal to say, the absence of any life within, the mechanical routine of everyday life, man sunk in his social background, no longer able to distinguish himself from it. The Smiths and the Martins no longer know how to talk because they no longer know how to think, they no longer know how to think because they are no longer capable of being moved, they have no passions, they no longer know how to be, they can become anyone or anything, for as they are no longer themselves, in an impersonal world, they can only be someone else, they are interchangeable: Martin can change places with Smith and vice versa, no one would notice the difference.[3]

When we recall that both Flora and Edward have seen the matchseller somewhere before, we understand that Barnabas is only the mirror in which they see their secret self reflected. Flora has led a sedate and shallow life tending her flowers when she would prefer to cultivate her budding passion. Barnabas provides her the opportunity to live out her fantasies as mistress and mother. Edward has a position of some importance and is likewise able to lead the good life outwardly. But he is empty within and he, like other hollow men, waits for someone to come and expose his emptiness. Barnabas merely provides the occasion for the removal of the bandages from Edward's weak eyes.

But finally it is not Barnabas that provides the occasion for revelation. It is Edward and Flora themselves. The river of language which courses from them reveals them more fully than any actions they might undertake. When one begins to hear the terrible silences between and behind their explosion of words, then he cannot help but understand the terrible silence which is at their center, the silence of emptiness. It is especially appropriate that language is the agent of moral revelation for, as Carlyle noted in *Past and Present*,

Speech is the gaseous element out of which most kinds of Practice and Performance, especially all kinds of moral Performance, condense themselves, and take shape; as the one is so will the other be.

After this emptiness has been revealed, what does one do? Edward, presumably, takes up selling matches; and Flora announces that while her husband is on the road for his company, she will be entertaining a houseguest. It would make a nice, tidy arrangement. But suppose that no Barnabas had entered the scene and supplanted one of the characters? Suppose the characters had come to realize the poverty of their own conditions, the emptiness of their own lives? Where do they go from there? If they are civilized people, civilization being an accommodation with the dark, a stylized barbarism, they will work out an accommodation of their own. *The Lover* (1963), originally a television play but converted to the stage, is "the tender love story" of Richard and Sarah who, after ten years of marriage and with the children away at boarding school, attempt to live in the presence of their own emptiness.

Richard is about to leave for the office when, after kissing his wife, he asks amiably, "Is your lover coming today?" Sarah replies, "Mmnn." Richard asks her how long she will be with her lover and, having learned that he should not return before six o'clock, pops off, wishing Sarah a pleasant afternoon. When Richard returns, he asks Sarah about her afternoon; and they chat pleasantly about her lover's visit. Finally Richard asks, though not in pique,

Does it ever occur to you that while you're spending the afternoon being unfaithful to me, I'm sitting at a desk going through balance sheets and graphs? (9)

When Sarah replies that she does not forget him entirely while she is with her lover, he seems pleased. After all she reminds him "it's you I love."

When Richard notices her high-heel shoes, the shoes she wore with her lover, he reminds her to change them. She apologizes, aware that she must stay within the rules of the frightful game they have devised. Richard enjoys the notion that his wife thought of him even while with her lover. But Sarah reminds him that she did not worry about him too much because she knew that he was with his mistress at the time. Richard disagrees, "I haven't got a mistress. I'm very well acquainted with a whore, but I haven't got a mistress. There's a world of difference . . . Just a common or garden slut. Not worth talking about. Handy between trains, nothing more" (11). Thus, Richard and Sarah congratulate themselves on their frankness, on their civilized arrangement.

When Sarah presses Richard to tell her about his companion, he replies that she is simply "a functionary who pleases or displeases" (12). Today she pleases, but perhaps tomorrow she will not. Richard seems to demand the quality of pure lust from his companion, hence the distinction between mistress and whore. Richard tells Sarah that he sought someone who was her opposite and that he could love her and still be drawn to "someone who could express and engender lust with all lust's cunning" (13). If he wants dignity and sensibility, he turns to his marriage, Richard explains; if he wants passion, he turns to his whore.

The continued probing for information about the other's lover begins to make the two a bit nervous. "Why all the questions," Richard asks. "Well, it was you who started it. Asking me so many questions about . . . my side of it. You don't normally do that," Sarah replies (14). The process of asking questions has once again endangered the delicate security which the characters have worked out. Questions lead to questions and Richard begins to wonder what would happen if he came home early one day or if the four of them got together for tea in the village. These suggestions unsettle Sarah; and she suggests to Richard that they leave things as they are because, as she explains, "I think things are beautifully balanced, Richard" (17).

The next day, after Richard has toddled off to the office, Sarah sits waiting for her lover. There is a knock at the door;

it is her lover! But it is only John the milkman. (John is the only other person to appear in the play.) He may, with his offer of cream and with the British associations with the name *John*, offer the same thing to Sarah that her lover offers. But Sarah sends him off, perhaps because he would not enhance the intellectual excitement of the game which is being played.

Finally, Max, her lover, appears; it is Richard with a suede jacket and no tie! He takes down a bongo drum and together they participate in an erotic charade. Within the game they play, there are several other games. Richard-Max pretends he has happened along to save Sarah from a molester. Her gratitude and his modesty is a model of propriety but soon he calls her Dolores and informs her that she cannot leave the hut. Sarah replies in mock horror,

> Trapped! I'm a married woman. You can't treat me like this.
> MAX [*moving to her*]   It's teatime, Mary. (23)

Sarah has maneuvered herself into a situation from which she cannot escape and therefore is ready to surrender without guilt. Richard-Max calls her by a number of different names suggesting perhaps the shifting roles she plays, but more importantly counterpointing his quest of the eternal seductress in her many guises.

After they have made love, Max casually asks about Richard, "I wonder if we'd get on. I wonder if we'd . . . you know . . . hit it off" (24). Sarah replies that she does not think so because the two men have little in common. Max wonders why Richard is so accommodating, why he puts up with Sarah's lover. Max complains that the arrangement is starting to weary him and that it cannot go on much longer. Sarah is disturbed, but Max-Richard says he wants to stop deceiving his wife. She thinks he only has a whore, he explains, and not a full-time mistress who is a "woman of grace, elegance, wit, imagination." Sarah protests that his wife does not mind, that she in fact is quite happy with the relationship.

Max persists, arguing that he ought to meet Richard and

have a sensible discussion of the whole business. Sarah grows panicky,

> Stop it! What's the matter with you? What's happened to you? [*quietly*] Please, please, stop it. What are you doing, playing a game?

MAX A game? I don't play games.

SARAH Don't you? You do. Oh, you do. You do. Usually I like them. (27)

But Max presses, explaining that he is through playing games. His mistress is too bony he explains. He prefers "voluminous great uddered feminine bullocks." Once, years earlier, he adds, she looked like that. Sarah believes Max is joking, playing a new variation on the old game; but as he leaves, Max protests that he is not joking.

When Richard returns, he asks Sarah if her lover came that day.

> Lover come?
> [*She does not reply*]
> Sarah?

SARAH What? Sorry. I was thinking of something.

RICHARD Did your lover come?

SARAH Oh yes. He came.

RICHARD In good shape?

SARAH I have a headache actually.

RICHARD Wasn't he in good shape?
> [*pause*]

SARAH We all have our off days.

RICHARD He, too? I thought the whole point of being a lover is that one didn't. I mean if I, for instance, were called upon to fulfil the function of a lover and felt disposed, shall we say, to accept the job, well, I'd as soon give it up as be found incapable of executing its proper and consistent obligation. (30)

Sarah's "diplomatic headache" is her effort to shunt Richard's painful questions aside. But Richard is in control of the situation and coolly pushes her toward the consummation of their game. The language he uses is that of the business world. The business world is the arena of social intercourse, the occasion for the exchange of wares, and most

importantly, a fictive community bound by rules and agree-
ments that are not so much "essential" as an accommodation
with need. In a broadly metaphoric way, then, the style and
subject of Richard's discourse is most appropriate to the
elaborately stylized arrangement which he and his partner
have worked out. Language, that most stylized of human
faculties, becomes the agent of destruction of their own
stylized arrangement.

The game is over Richard insists. He tells Sarah that her
"debauchery," her "illegitimate lust" is finished. Sarah asks
him if he would like some cold ham, but her ploy fails.
Richard wonders why it took him ten years of marriage to
recognize his ignominious position. He will no longer permit
his wife to consort with her lover in his living room. Furthermore, he announces, he has gotten rid of his whore because
she was too bony. Sarah is confused and desperate. Richard
seems to be calling an end to the game that has kept them
going, the "vital lie" that has sustained their marriage.

SARAH   But you liked . . . you said you liked . . . Richard
. . . but you love me . . .
RICHARD   Of course.
SARAH   Yes . . . you love me . . . you don't mind him . . .
you understand him . . . don't you? . . . I mean, you
know better than I do . . . darling . . . all's well . . .
all's well . . . the evenings . . . and the afternoons . . .
do you see? Listen, I do have dinner for you. It's ready.
I wasn't serious. It's Boeuf bourgignon. And tomorrow I'll
have Chicken Chasseur. Would you like it? (36)

The pauses in her conversation suggest her frantic confusion
and her inability even now to bring the game out into the
open and, perhaps, devise a new set of ground rules.

Richard then nonchalantly picks up the bongo drum and
questions her about it. Sarah replies,

> [*with quiet anguish*] You've no right to question me. No
> right at all. It was our arrangement. No questions of this
> kind. Please. Don't, don't. It was our arrangement. (37)

Richard, in feigning innocence over the significance of the
bongo drum, still keeps one foot in the game even while he is

in the process of destroying that game. Out of her desperate need to keep Richard from ending the game, Sarah claims that she has other lovers besides Max. Richard cannot know whether she is fabricating or not but if John the milkman is any example, it is extremely unlikely that she does have other lovers.

Richard begins scratching and thumping the drum. He tells Sarah that her husband will not mind. Sarah is confused. She plays the game with Max but this is Richard. He reminds her that she is trapped, that she cannot escape. She wonders what her husband would say if he knew. The play ends with Richard whispering in her ear "you lovely whore."

Richard's effort to merge the various personae: wife, mistress, and whore constitutes the primary motivation of the play. Richard and Sarah have perceived the emptiness of their relationship and have sought to revitalize it by playing a rather interesting little game, a game that provides them with the excitement and sense of adventure which their relationship can no longer supply. The game takes its mode of expression in sexual terms but the play is more than a variation on the old skin game with perhaps a few pirandellian twists here and there. The game is their effort to revitalize their whole existence and sex is but a part of that existence. Richard and Sarah are trying to save themselves before they become Edward and Flora.

The game gives them, as with the assorted patrons of Genet's *The Balcony,* the illusion of significance. In their recharged sexual potency their lives take on new meaning. But the game alone is not enough. Richard has the courage to face the ultimate bankruptcy of the game. He asks the leading questions which Sarah fears because she cannot conceive of life without this unifying fiction. Richard is not really so tired of the game that he wants to end it forever. He would prefer to incorporate the excitement of the game into their daily lives. At the end of the play the borderline between the game and the everyday reality grows fuzzy, and Sarah becomes a "lovely whore" without ceasing to be his wife as well.

The game has made it possible for Richard and Sarah to

express their deepest needs; it has been their language when language was inadequate as a vehicle of meaningful expression. The conclusion presents two people who have finally awakened to their deepest desires. They have found, among other things, an atavistic violence as a part of their sexuality, a violence in which one is master and one mastered. They have long needed to express this facet of their nature but have repressed its unsettling character and have sublimated it as a stylized encounter within a set of rules. The central rule has always been: do not confuse the roles played. Richard's wisdom is to see that the roles must merge if they are to survive the game. Before, the game had been a cerebral justification of a physical need, an intellectual stratagem to keep the peace. But at the end Richard and Sarah are perhaps, and with Pinter one must always conclude with a perhaps, ready to learn the anarchic delights of carnal knowledge.

When Richard speaks of his afternoon at the office, we know that he is speaking of his afternoon with Sarah. He knows it; she knows it; and we know it; therefore, the usual irony is not intended here. The irony arises in the bankruptcy of a game that was created to save a bankrupt relationship. But it is in the ending of the game that Richard and Sarah recover the possibilities of playing life for keeps. Wellwarth has observed that "They can achieve physical communication only through an elaborate bypassing of emotional communication." [4] Ironically, however, it is the failure of their sexual communication that occasions the possibility of a more profound emotional communication.

The Lover, then, is not another rendition of the "failure of communication" theme so dear to postwar dramatists. Pinter has expressed his feelings about that theme,

We have heard many times that tired, grimy phrase: "Failure of communication" . . . and this phrase has been fixed to my work quite consistently. I believe the contrary. I think that we communicate only too well, in our silence, in what is unsaid, and that what takes place is a continual evasion, desperate rear guard attempts to keep ourselves to ourselves. Communication is too alarming. To enter into someone else's life is too frightening. To disclose to others the poverty within us is too fearsome a possibility.[5]

The game has provided Richard and Sarah an elaborate device for not only expressing something they are unable to express but, more importantly, to withhold something vital from each other. Their problem is to come to know their own deepest self and that of the other more fully (and the game has helped them to do that), and finally to learn to live without the game. They need to confront the poverty of their relationship, even the poverty of the self which they bring to each other and go on from there. The most crucial line of the play is Sarah's protest, "but it's you I love" (10). Behind the contrived rhetoric of the game, the still, small voice of her deepest hope emerges. Out of the noisy collapse of the game, the silent gesture of reconciliation emerges.

3

The Struggle for Possession
The Collection, The Caretaker

Pinter returns repeatedly to several themes which, expressed in problematic terms, seem central to the articulation of his vision. The problem of verification, for example, remains crucial to all of his plays. Is room seven empty or not? Does Rose really know Riley? Who are Goldberg and McCann and what is the source of their strange power over Stanley? Who is the party upstairs giving such absurd orders? The problem of identity recurs as well. Who is the matchseller or who, for that matter, is Edward? Who is the real husband of Sarah—Richard or Max? The questions continue but the answers are not forthcoming. These themes are merged in some of Pinter's later plays as *a struggle for possession*. The struggle is to find and possess the truth, or as Kierkegaard might say, to stand in absolute relationship to it. But the struggle is also to find and possess the real person, the embodiment of the truth. *The Caretaker* merges these themes and is perhaps Pinter's masterpiece thus far. But before we consider *The Caretaker*, it may be helpful to examine *The Collection* which was written the year after *The Caretaker*. *The Collection* is admittedly cast in a minor key, but it also picks up and magnifies one of the leitmotivs of *The Caretaker*.

The title of *The Collection* (1961) is polysemous. The play naturally involves a collection of people. Two of those characters, Bill and Stella, have been to the showing of a collection of dresses in another city. But perhaps the most important implication suggests that there is a collection of truths.[1] *The Collection* is a semicomic exploration of the old prob-

[*pause*]
If you let me get up . . .
[*pause*]
I'm not very comfortable.
[*pause*]
If you let me get up . . . I'll . . . I'll tell you . . . the truth . . . (58)

The "truth" that Bill proclaims is that he met Stella in the elevator when she was accidentally thrown into his arms. They kissed and then parted. James supplements with his version, reminding Bill that he took a bath in her bathroom and sang "Coming through the Rye." James had phoned at this time and he asks Bill if he was sitting next to her on the bed while she talked to her husband. Bill denies sitting there; he was, rather, lying on the bed. The multiple versions of the story suggest that someone is lying, but then there may also be multiple truths which each character can honestly affirm.[2]

Pinter continues to shift rapidly back and forth between the two apartments. It is clear that Harry resents the visit of James. He suspects that James has usurped some of the power over Bill that Harry covets. James, at the same time, is telling Stella that he wants to have a word with "the other man," not telling her that he already has met Bill. Stella protests that Bill does not matter to her and James wonders if it could have been anyone.

STELLA   Of course it couldn't have been anyone. It was him. It was just . . . something . . .
JAMES   That's what I mean. It was him. That's why I think he's worth having a look at. I want to see what he's like. It'll be instructive, educational. (65)

John Russell Taylor has suggested that James is not out to find the truth about the sleeping-in incident; he rather wants to know more about his wife, to discover what kind of person she would tumble into bed with after a casual encounter.[3] But James is also, and more importantly, engaged in a search for himself, for the kind of man whom his wife can spurn so easily. In order to find the truth about himself, he must paradoxically recover or lose Stella. The struggle with Bill for possession of Stella is then the token of the struggle for the truth of their relationship.

But there is another twist to the truth that James is uncovering. He is discovering that Bill is attractive to him as well. Thus the struggle for possession emerges from another angle, another variation on the old *ménage à trois*. Accordingly, James finds himself sympathizing with Stella about how she might have found Bill attractive.

> Well I do understand, but only after meeting him. Now I'm perfectly happy. I can see it both ways, three ways, all ways . . . every way. It's perfectly clear, there's nothing to it, everything's back to normal. The only difference is that I've come across a man I can respect. It isn't often you can do that, that that happens, and really I suppose I've got you to thank. (66)

James admits now that he can see the truth from a different perspective. He concludes by telling Stella that she has opened up a whole new world for him.

On James' second visit to Bill's flat, the two men engage in a round of verbal sparring which culminates in their conclusion that one can best learn something about himself by looking in the mirror. Bill thinks mirrors lie but James argues that they tell the truth. The two stand together in the reflection of the mirror, and the truth which is latent in their relationship emerges.

At the same time James and Bill are meeting, Harry has gone round to see Stella, also to learn the truth. Harry wants to get at the truth because he senses that he is losing his power over Bill to James. After he reveals that he picked Bill out of the slums and set him up as a dress designer, Stella admits that the whole story of the encounter in Leeds is James' fabrication. James has been overworked of late, she explains.

In the other apartment Bill and James are playfully sparring with a knife. Bill wants James to hold the blade and explains that it will not hurt him if he grasps it firmly. James picks up a knife and challenges Bill to a duel. He tosses a knife to Bill who is slightly cut just as Harry returns. In playing with the knife, James and Bill have tried to articulate in a non-linguistic fashion the nature of their attraction to each other. The knife is a phallic metonymy for the sexual attraction which has brought them together just as the cylindrical phone booth upstage served as the agent of association in the Stella-Bill relationship. Both times, as caller and as knife thrower, James has found himself in the position of "making contact" with Bill, the only person who can tell him the truth of either relationship.

Harry announces that Stella has confessed her fabrication. When James asks Bill why he confirmed her story, Bill explains, "You wanted me to confirm it. It amused me to do so" (77). Bill, Harry explains, is just a boy from the slums and agreeing to such nonsense is his idea of a good time. Harry continues his diatribe against his protégé,

> There's nothing wrong with slugs, in their place, but he's a slum slug, there's nothing wrong with slum slugs in their place, but this one won't keep his place, he crawls all over the walls of nice houses, leaving slime, don't you boy? He confirms stupid sordid little stories just to amuse himself, while everyone else has to run round in circles to get to the root of the matter and smooth the whole thing out. All he can do is sit and suck his bloody hand and decompose like the filthy putrid slum slug he is. What about another whisky, Horne? (78)

Harry's strategy is aimed at one end—to recover Bill. To recover his lover, he must degrade Bill so that James will not be attracted to him, he must destroy Stella's story so that James can have someone to return to, and he must reestablish his domination of Bill.

James apologizes for the inconvenience of his wife's lie; and he imputes fatigue, the same justification she had attempted on his behalf. But as James leaves, Bill says that he and Stella only sat in the lounge for two hours and talked about going up to her room. Thus the betrayal becomes manifest once again. James stands in stunned silence before returning home to renew the cycle of questions. He asks Stella what really happened in Leeds, but Stella sits in silence with a sphinx-like smile on her face.

The Collection, then, is a collection of stratagems to get at the truth. In the course of the play, the testimonies of Stella, Bill, and James have been contradicted. By its conclusion one no longer suspects, or particularly cares, that there may be a single, specific truth. Everyone professes interest in the truth but only James is intimately involved. Harry only wants to get to the truth in order to regain Bill and he would probably accept any lie that served the same purpose. But James needs to know the truth about Stella and the truth about Bill in order to know the truth about himself. He is not so much interested, then, in seeking leads about Leeds as he is interested in confronting his rightful image in the mirror.

If the adultery did take place, then both couples have been subverted. The traditional associations of the cuckold's horns with James Horne and the Devil's power over the souls of men with the aging homosexual Harry Cain hardly seem to function in *The Collection.* Rather, the sexual theme remains only a part of the larger quest for the truth of himself in which James is engaged. James and Bill seem to be in a struggle for the possession of Stella. If James can recover Stella, he can recover his virile image of himself. But James and Harry also seem to be struggling for the possession of that truth embodied by Bill. In the course of his association with Bill, James discovers his latent homosexuality. Again, the person asking questions finds himself in an exposed position.

The sexual relationships of this play, extramarital and homosexual, are articulated in metonymic forms. The phone booth stands at the center of the stage and at the center of the connection between the characters. The knife, a lesser though perhaps more potent image, becomes the external object upon which Bill and James project their unspoken relationship. Similarly the mirror reveals the truth of their relationship to them when they are incapable of recognizing it by themselves. In each case Pinter has tried to make communication possible under awkward and painful circumstances. The silent gesture, the parry with the knife, permits the characters to go beyond the limitations of language.

Arnold Hinchliffe has further suggested that the play depicts characters who are trying to rethink the nature of their relationships. This larger pattern of reflection is thus echoed in numerous lesser incidents where, for example, James reconsiders his distaste for olives and Bill reconsiders his usual liking for potatoes.[4] Such supportive details may seem trivial, and are, but they are not therefore irrelevant to the larger course of the work.

In an early television script *Night School* (1960), Pinter depicted the return of Walter to his home after a term in prison. Walter soon learns that his room has been let to Sally, a nice young schoolteacher. He sets out to recover his room and to learn the truth about Sally. Ultimately he learns that she is also a night-club hostess. He finally regains his room and its attendant security, but he loses Sally and never fully learns the truth about her. In *Night School* the search for security and the search for truth are fused in Walter's attempt to recover his room. These themes which preoccupy Pinter—the room as a haven from the threatening world outside, the search for the truth, the quest for identity, and the struggle for possession—attain their most engaging synthesis in *The Caretaker*. *Night School* and *The Collection* thus serve as five-finger exercises for what most observers agree to be Pinter's greatest achievement.

Pascal's contention that "we wander in times which are not ours" evokes the recurrent pattern of exile and estrangement in Western literature. The number of allusions to a quest, a journey, or to "tramping" about in *The Caretaker* (1960) suggests that it partakes of this tradition.[5] The end of the quest is the golden fleece, the pot of gold, or the fair princess, tokens of material and spiritual identity. The three careworn characters of *The Caretaker* are at various junctures along the circuitous path of this quest for identity. The "status" they seek is then to achieve some "standing" (*Dastehen, Dasein,*), some high "station," some "stature" to be reckoned with, some "understanding" of the mysteries of their existence.

Aston, a man in his thirties, brings Davies, an elderly tramp, back to his flat. The room is a chaotic assemblage of junk including, literally, the kitchen sink. Aston finds a chair amidst the rubble and offers it to Davies. Davies replies,

> Sit down? Huh . . . I haven't had a good sit down . . . I haven't had a proper sit down . . . well, I couldn't tell you. (7)

Davies' stumbling, the gaps in his rhetoric, the continual restatement, and the admission of his failure to communicate in even this simple, introductory comment, illustrate Pinter's strategy throughout the play. Richard Schechner has rightly noted that much of the play is an elaborate put-on and "the whole play is built around the non-exchange of information." [6]

We have earlier seen Stanley at the mercy of Goldberg and McCann, and Davies also finds himself in a position where he does not know what kind of game is being played or where its drift and direction will take him. For example, when Davies asks why Aston is laboring over a toaster plug, Aston remarks with gravity that it does not work. Davies knows that the plug does not work or Aston would not be tinkering with it. He is really asking another kind of question and is frustrated by having his overt and obvious question answered. At the end of the first act, Aston's brother, Mick, sums up the business, "What's the game?" (29). Davies spends the rest of his time trying to tumble to the shifting rules of the game.

Davies feels he owes his benefactor an explanation, an *apologia pro vita sua*, a justification for being a derelict. He complains of the "aliens" who have given him a bad time. The Poles, the Greeks, the blacks, have mistreated him, and he has nearly come to blows with them. Aston is extremely taciturn and shows no outward interest in Davies' *apologia*; he again suggests that Davies sit down and rest from his travel. Davies replies,

> Yes, but what I got to do first, you see, what I got to do, I got to loosen myself up, you see what I mean? (8)

Davies' "loosening up" takes form in his incessant chatter and persiflage, a baroque exfoliation of language that reveals in its attempt to conceal the insecurity of an anxious, grubby little tramp. Davies' torrent of words is especially noticeable when juxtaposed against the silence of Aston. Aston's reticence discomfits the tramp who cannot bear the silence of his spaces.

As Davies pokes about the cluttered room, taking stock of his new environment, he confronts a statuette of Buddha, a statuette Aston bought because he thought it well made. He then regards Aston's bed and observes how it gets rather drafty when the wind blows outside. Aston's responses are minimal and noncommittal. Davies is particularly unsettled to learn that a family of "blacks" lives next door, but pleased to learn that Aston is in charge of the house. The survey Davies takes, the questions he asks are designed to acquaint himself with his temporary home, his home away from home. No detail is insignificant to Davies. A bed that is too close to the window is a reminder of the times he has slept in the gutter. His proximity to the "blacks" reminds him that he is never too far from those who would do him in if they got a chance. The composite portrait of Davies which emerges from such insignificant details is that of a man who has been homeless and rootless and now sees the possibility of finding a home and taking root.

Davies does not reveal much more information to Aston than Aston reveals to Davies. Nevertheless, one of the seemingly insignificant details that forms part of a larger pattern may be observed in Davies' preoccupation with shoes. For example, Davies asks Aston if he has a spare pair of shoes.

ASTON   Shoes?
DAVIES   Them bastards at the monastery let me down again.
ASTON   [*going to his bed*]: Where?
DAVIES   Down at Luton. Monastery down at Luton. . . . I
    got a mate at Shepherd's Bush, you see. . . .
ASTON   [*looking under his bed*]: I might have a pair. (13)

Through the process of circumlocution, Aston returns to the subject of shoes after stopping for a moment on the subject of the monastery. Through a similar, though more radical process of circumlocution, Davies is really thinking of the quest again. The right pair of shoes will make the continuation of his journey possible. Davies is particularly peeved with the monks to whom he went for a handout, but the monks would give him only a meal. Aston turns up an old pair, but Davies declares that they do not fit him correctly. Beggars, it seems, can sometimes be choosers. If we wander in times which are not ours, Davies refuses to wander in shoes whose size is not his. Davies has already begun to think on the room as a home, a way station, a hiatus from the rigors of the journey; thus he is not overly eager to be fitted with shoes. When Aston asks him to stay over, Davies feigns indecision but quickly agrees.

Davies professes hope that the weather will break and that he will be able to get down to Sidcup because, as he explains,

> I got my papers there!
> [*pause*]
> ASTON   Your what?
> DAVIES   I got my papers there!
> [*pause*]
> ASTON   What are they doing at Sidcup?
> DAVIES   A man I know has got them. I left them with him. You see? They prove who I am! I can't move without them papers. They tell you who I am. You see! I'm stuck without them. (19)

Davies is in search of his identity. Someone down in Sidcup has papers which prove who he is. In order to continue his wandering about, he must get his papers. Davies is traveling under an assumed name, Bernard Jenkins; and it has been fifteen years since he has had his papers. For the same reason that Davies cannot find a suitable pair of shoes, one suspects that he will never be able to get to Sidcup either.

Because of the sounds he made in his sleep, Davies is asked the next morning whether he suffered nightmares. You were jabbering, Aston tells him.

> DAVIES   I don't jabber, man. Nobody ever told me that before.
> [*pause*]

What would I be jabbering about?
ASTON   I don't know.
DAVIES   I mean, where's the sense in it?
    [*pause*]
    Nobody ever told me that before.
    [*pause*]
    You got hold of the wrong bloke, mate.
ASTON   [*crossing to the bed with the toaster*]: No. You woke
    me up. I thought you might have been dreaming.
DAVIES   I wasn't dreaming. I never had a dream in my life.
    [*pause*] (22, 23)

Davies is afraid that he might have talked too much,
revealed himself, made himself known. He bristles with the
thought that Aston may have a negative appraisal of him. He
concludes by suggesting that perhaps the noises were from
the blacks, the aliens ever willing to do him a bad turn.

Aston tries to learn a bit more about his guest and questions him further.

ASTON   What did you say your name was?
DAVIES   Bernard Jenkins is my assumed one.
ASTON   No, your other one?
DAVIES   Davies. MacDavies.
ASTON   Welsh, are you?
DAVIES   Eh?
ASTON   You Welsh?
    [*pause*]
DAVIES   Well, I been around, you know . . . what I mean
    . . . I been about . . .
ASTON   Where were you born then?
DAVIES   [*darkly*]: What do you mean?
ASTON   Where were you born?
DAVIES   I was . . . uh . . . oh, it's a bit hard, like, to set
    your mind back . . . see what I mean . . . going back.
    . . . a good way . . . lose a bit of track, like . . . you
    know. . . . (25)

Davies seems rootless, without a history or stable identity.
His isolation is conveyed by his evasive answers to the questions. All identifying details seem lost and one wonders if
Davies has ever known where he came from. The halting
phrases, the confused pauses betray his fragmented consciousness. Davies has lost his way. He cannot retrace his

steps or begin anew. Somewhere, in Sidcup perhaps, he may recover the papers which prove who he is but one ought not to be expected to go to Sidcup in ill-fitting shoes or in nasty British winters.

After Aston has left the flat, Davies pokes about by himself. Suddenly he is attacked and thrown to the floor by Aston's younger brother, Mick, who has entered unseen. "What's the game?" Mick asks. Davies is completely terrified by the sudden attack and replies "Nothing, nothing. Nothing" (30). When Mick asks him his name, Davies does not, and perhaps cannot, answer. But ironically he refuses to answer because he does not know Mick's name. Quickly Mick turns his threatening appearance into a polite concern for how well Davies slept the night before. It is this constant shifting from menace to courtesy and back again that keeps Davies unsettled by Mick. Davies might well ask Mick what the game is.

Mick begins the second act with a number of loose flowing recollections about acquaintances who are brought to mind by Davies. Mick's long monologues at first seem to interrupt the narrative flow (such as it is), but they rather intensify the relationship between the characters. Though the monologues seem digressions they are intimately related to the care and feeding of Davies by his new keepers. Furthermore, his resemblance to other people are additional occasions when Davies' own identity is confused or called into question.

Mick keeps at Davies, probing, questioning, and driving the tramp to distraction. Davies is frightened of Mick because he senses the hostility that lurks behind Mick's solicitousness. Mick carefully pronounces Davies' putative name "Jen . . . kins." His care in pronouncing each syllable indicates his incredulity and his disdain. Thus the most innocent questions upset Davies and thrust him off balance. Mick repeats his questions.

> [*a shout*] Sleep here last night?
> DAVIES Yes . . .
> MICK [*continuing at a great pace*]: How'd you sleep?
> DAVIES I slept—

MICK   Sleep well?
DAVIES   Now look—
MICK   What bed?
DAVIES   That—
MICK   Not the other?
DAVIES   No!
MICK   Choosy.
   [pause]
   [quietly] Choosy.
   [pause]
   [again amiable] What sort of sleep did you have in that
   bed?
DAVIES   [banging the floor]: All right!
MICK   You weren't uncomfortable?
DAVIES   [groaning]: All right! (33)

Soon Davies is at the mercy of Mick's interrogation even as
Stanley was psychologically terrorized and humbled by Goldberg and McCann.

Mick's interrogation concludes with a long harangue in
which he concludes that Davies is an old robber and is
stinking up the place. But then he subtly offers to rent the
flat to the tramp provided Davies can produce sufficient
collateral. Mick's harangue is slowly transformed into a verbal labyrinth of technical real-estate and banking terms
which Davies could not possibly understand. By the end of
Mick's speech, Davies is totally shattered. Mick has spun a
maze of language in which he, like Goldberg, has been
saying nothing but saying it well. Davies' stature is thus
reduced again because he realizes that he is being manipu-
lated by Mick. Mick's parting shot is to ask the tramp about
his bank, but Davies' unstable financial standing is only
another reminder of his questionable standing as a human
being. The verbal outburst by Mick is quite humorous insofar as it is filled with nonsense and based on *non-sequiturs*,
but the effect on Davies is something else. As Pinter noted in
an essay, "more often than not the speech only *seems* to be
funny—the man in question is actually fighting a battle for
his life." [7]

Aston's return to the flat concludes Mick's dalliance with

Davies and the two brothers move off to a different language game. They do not seem to be malicious in their intention, but the effect on Davies is the same. He finds himself always the outsider and is never quite certain whether they are having one on him or he is simply missing the point. In regard to a leak in the ceiling Mick observes,

> You still got that leak.
> ASTON   Yes.
>   [*pause*]
>   It's coming from the roof. . . .
> MICK   You're going to tar it over?
> ASTON   Yes.
> MICK   What?
> ASTON   The cracks.
>   [*pause*]
> MICK   You'll be tarring over the cracks on the roof.
> ASTON   Yes.
>   [*pause*]
> MICK   Think that'll do it?
> ASTON   It'll do it, for the time being.
> MICK   Uh.
>   [*pause*]
> DAVIES   [*abruptly*]: . . . What do you do . . . ?
>   [*They both look at him.*]
>   What do you do . . . when that bucket's full?
>   [*pause*]
> ASTON   Empty it.
>   [*pause*] (37)

Even the most banal aspects of existence seem fraught with serious implications for Davies because he is trying desperately to learn the game so that he can play it too. At every turn, however, he is defeated by language. Language is either too much for him or not enough for him; it either bewilders him or tells him the obvious. Either way he does not communicate to others nor understand fully what they are saying to him.

Because of the confusion about his own identity, about his "standing" in the world, Davies does not trust language at all. He cannot bring himself to say what he wants to say and so stammers around the subject. When Aston offers Davies a job as caretaker for the house, Davies needs to feel out the implications of such a responsibility; but he is unsure how he should proceed.

DAVIES Well, I reckon . . . Well, I'd have to know . . . you know. . . .
ASTON What sort of. . . .
DAVIES Yes, what sort of . . . you know. . . .
       [*pause*]
ASTON Well, I mean. . . .
DAVIES I mean, I'd have to . . . I'd have to. . . .
ASTON Well, I could tell you. . . .
DAVIES That's . . . that's it . . . you see . . . you get my meaning?
ASTON When the time comes. . . .
DAVIES I mean, that's what I'm getting at, you see. . . .
ASTON More or less exactly what you. . . .
DAVIES You see, what I mean to say . . . what I'm getting at is . . . I mean, what sort of jobs. . . .
       [*pause*]
ASTON Well, there's things like the stairs . . . and the . . . the bells. . . .
DAVIES But it'd be a matter . . . wouldn't it . . . it'd be a matter of a broom . . . isn't it?
ASTON Yes, and of course, you'd need a few brushes.
DAVIES You'd need implements . . . you see . . . you'd need a good few implements. . . . (42, 43)

Davies' continual need to define, to make certain he knows all the variables is the natural response of a man so insecure that he is trying to order his life, to draw up a contract for it so that he knows how the parties of the first and second part will act. His effort to know all the terms of his contract is the initial reflex of a man who does not know himself. If he cannot know himself, he may at least know his terrain; he may at least establish a few points of reference so that he will know what he is getting into. When Aston explains that in addition to cleaning up, Davies could answer any queries that might come to the door, Davies is frightened. One never knows who is likely to come to the door; and he, like Rose and Stanley, cannot be too careful when it comes to confronting strangers. The irony of selecting a man to answer questions who cannot answer his own questions is not wholly lost on Davies. Furthermore, he concludes, to take on the position of caretaker would be to take on a fixed identity for a spell. He is worried that then people would "have him in"; they would be able to deal with him and maybe even discover that his name is not really "Jen . . . kins."

In the following scene Mick also offers Davies the position of caretaker. When Mick asks for references, Davies explains that he has his papers at Sidcup and that he plans to go there soon to get them. Thus the scene with Mick parallels the scene with Aston, but Davies now begins to wonder which one of the brothers is really controlling the game. Davies is nevertheless slowly drawn to align himself with Mick, at first because Mick seems the more dynamic, and the more frightening, of the two brothers; but later Davies learns some reason for Aston's taciturnity and he is thereby able to "get the goods" on Aston and use the information for leverage against the older brother.

In the longest speech of the play, the conclusion to the second act, Aston utilizes well over a thousand painfully chosen words to fill in his background. He is perhaps the only Pinter character who reveals his background so totally. Aston concludes that his problem was that he talked too much, that he revealed too much of himself. He forgot that language is more often used to conceal rather than reveal one's feelings. As a result Aston was institutionalized. When his "complaint" was diagnosed, he was lobotomized and has never been the same since. In halting, emotionally flat tones Aston explains that he wants to go back out into the world and get the man who put the pincers on his skull. But first he wants to build a shed in the garden. Aston's preoccupation with carpentry and tools may be understood as part of his effort to deal with a piece of reality that he can handle. His expertise with tools somehow belies his awkwardness in the world outside the flat. His visions have been canceled by the world so he retreats to a more inoffensive kind of creativity. He becomes a handyman, a man handy about the house, a house boy.

Act two represents the fulcrum of the play. It is the

occasion in which the triangular relationship begins to take shape and in which Davies begins to try to play the game. The act begins with Mick baiting Davies by asking the tramp's name three times. Then, through a process of circumlocution and *non-sequitur*, Mick springs a trap on Davies. Mick knows all the answers ahead of time and merely uses the questions to push Davies to the brink of disintegration. Both brothers offer Davies the caretaker position, and the tramp begins to wonder with whom he ought to align himself. The act ends with the confession by Aston and Davies' choice seems clear. He will align himself with the stronger against the weaker. He will, if he can swing it, become number two in the house instead of number three.

Act three fittingly begins with Davies and Mick planning for the future. Mick has grandiose schemes for redecorating the run-down flat, for transforming the slum dwelling into a "palace." Davies in the meantime complains about the older brother. Aston does not say much, Davies asserts, and he lets the "blacks" get away with too much. But Davies' effort to supplant Aston receives a blow when he asks Mick about the "palace."

DAVIES Who would live there?
MICK I would. My brother and me. (61)

The rejection is unspoken but Davies realizes that he is still an outsider and that he will have to try harder. He continues his attack on Aston while he praises Mick. "He's no friend of mine," he says of Aston. "You don't know where you are with him. I mean, with a bloke like you, you know where you are" (61). The repeated phrases again betray Davies' anxiety over the need to know where he is, to know where he "stands."

When Aston interrupts, proffering another pair of shoes, Davies sees that they have no laces; and he observes to Aston, with considerably more sarcasm than he was capable of initially, that he cannot very well get down to Sidcup in shoes with no laces. Davies realizes that his security depends on his acceptance in the house and he begins to threaten Aston.

They can put the pincers on your head again, man! They can have them on again! Any time. All they got to do is get the word. They'd carry you in there, boy. They'd come here and pick you up and carry you in! They'd keep you fixed. They'd put them pincers on your head, they'd have you fixed! (67)

To this threat Aston calmly replies, "I don't think we're hitting it off." He suggests that Davies find another place to live, but Davies has smelled blood and demands that Aston leave. The tramp is sure that he and Mick have an understanding and that, even though Aston has told him to leave, he is in the stronger position.

When Davies turns to enlist Mick's help in supplanting Aston, the tramp is told that he is an imposter. Mick says that he is only interested in Davies as an interior decorator. Davies claims that he was hired as a caretaker and not an interior decorator. Mick concludes, "You're a bloody imposter, mate!" (72). Mick's judgment is both a factual and a moral judgment. Davies does not know who he is; he is Davies playing the role of "Jen . . . kins" and he is a caretaker who is expected to be an interior decorator. Thus Davies is sensitive to the charge and flails out, "you start calling me names—"

MICK   What is your name?
DAVIES   Don't start that—
MICK   No, what's your real name?
DAVIES   My real name's Davies.
MICK   What's the name you go under?
DAVIES   Jenkins!
MICK   You got two names. What about the rest? Eh? Now come on, why did you tell me all this dirt about you being an interior decorator?
DAVIES   I didn't tell you nothing! Won't you listen to what I'm saying?
         [pause] (72, 73)

Davies has been unable to say what he wants to say and therefore does not want to be held accountable for what Mick thinks he may have said. Mick pushes Davies, reminding him that "I can take nothing you say at face value. Every

word you speak is open to any number of different interpretations. Most of what you say is lies" (73). Furthermore, Mick
adds pointedly, Davies has never seemed in much of a hurry
to get down to Sidcup to get his papers.

Mick hurls the Buddha against the stove. He has other
things besides Davies to worry about, he explains. Mick's
destruction of the Buddha, his brother's possession, is a tacit
assent to some of Davies' criticisms of Aston. For all his
self-possession Mick apparently has his own insecurities, the
most notable of which is how to take care of his invalid
brother. Mick even wonders whether he ought to pack up
and move on to something else.

Now that he has been rejected by Mick, Davies tries once
more to make up to Aston. He announces himself willing to
make compromises, but it is clear that neither Mick nor
Aston wants anything to do with him. Davies stands before
Aston and in his shambling way confronts the abyss before
him. In the silences of his speech, one may fathom the
labored breathing of a destroyed man.

> Where am I going to go?
> [*pause*]
> If you want me to go . . . I'll go. You just say the word.
> [*pause*]
> I'll tell you what though . . . them shoes . . . them shoes
> you give me . . . they're working out all right . . . they're
> all right. Maybe I could . . . get down . . .
> [*Aston remains still, his back to him, at the window*]
> Listen . . . if I . . . got down . . . if I was to . . . get
> my papers . . . would you . . . would you let . . . would
> you . . . if I got down . . . and got my. . . .
> [*long silence*]
>   [*Curtain*]

Each of the characters of *The Caretaker* nurses a private
illusion. Davies wants to get to Sidcup to find his papers and
substantiate his identity. Aston wants to build the shed in
the back as a first step in his return to the world. Mick wants
to turn the shabby flat into a palace. His illusions are a bit
more subtle but no less indicative of his similarity to the
others. Each wants to make his way in the world. While

Aston and Mick are important to the story, it is clear that Davies is the central character. Davies lacks the strength or the wit to go it alone, however; thus he must necessarily make alliances. His is the will to power without the power. Mick has intelligence and Aston has a kind of brute strength. If Davies can effect either alliance, he will have a winning combination of either intelligence and will or strength and will. But Davies oversteps himself; for if Mick were asked whether he was his brother's keeper, he would still have to give a reluctant assent. Davies might well have been able to work out a *modus vivendi* with the two of them, but his insecurity pushes him too far. If Davies were merely crushed by the others, his plight would be only pathetic. But he seeks to crush in turn and is not unwilling to turn on Aston, the rather helpless creature who took him off the street in the first place. Nevertheless, however much the viciousness of Davies may alienate us, Esslin only slightly exaggerates when he observes that Davies' unsuccessful plea for a home "assumes almost the cosmic proportions of Adam's expulsion from Paradise." [8]

Davies is more buffoon than tragic hero, yet there are aspects of his character that approximate the classical *hamartia*. His "flaw" is to miscalculate, to misread the silent communion between brother and brother. With mock paternalism, Mick warns Davies rather early that he is about to miscalculate.

> Watch your step, sonny! You're knocking at the door when no one's at home. Don't push it too hard. You come busting into a private house, laying your hands on anything you can lay your hands on. Don't overstep the mark, son. (38)

Davies also miscalculates when he assumes that he is clever enough to master someone else's game. However, Davies never breaks into the other's game; he remains the outsider. In *The Guest*, the film version of *The Caretaker*, Mick's baiting of Davies goes one step further when he picks Davies up in his truck and threatens to drive him to Sidcup. Instead he drives around a traffic island and lets Davies out at the same spot they started. To Davies' consternation, his hand had nearly been forced; but Mick resolves the threat in a fashion which suggests that he has long tumbled to the particular game that Davies has been playing.

The apartment of *The Caretaker* may be seen as an expanded version of "the room." This time, however, the intruder is not the threat but the one threatened. It is the intruder who is seeking a room, an indefinite pause in his quixotic quest for Sidcup. Davies is trying to find what the brothers already seem to have—an identity concretized by their own home. It is not much of a home, to be sure; but it is a useful labyrinthine barrier against intruders like Davies who want to enter, divide, and conquer but instead become hopelessly bewildered. Such an analysis overlooks the insecurity of Aston and Mick, however. Simply to have a flat is not to be secure as the characters of *The Room*, *The Birthday Party*, *the Dumb Waiter*, and *A Slight Ache* have so abundantly illustrated. The condition of Aston and Mick, then, is quantitatively not qualitatively superior to that of Davies.

Aston, for example, seems the only decent, that is kind and gentle, character in the play. One suspects that he was no different before his experience in the hospital, that the talking he was doing, the disturbance he was making was perhaps a plea for peace or compassion or more likely the right to be left alone to do his own work. But in the institution he was violated. He was held down while the ministries of social love were communicated to him by the man with the pincers. Aston's lobotomy represents one of Pinter's rare decisions to concretize the horror which a character may sense but not identify. But we must again resist the temptation to allegorize and to see Aston as Pinter's symbol of protest against the dehumanizing forces in the world. Pinter specifically observes that he had "no axe to grind" with the character of Aston and that we should not take everything he says about the hospital as necessarily true.[9]

Mick and Davies, on the other hand, are safe from the institution, for their forms of madness are consonant with the madness of their culture and they are accordingly rather normal citizens. It is chilling to wonder how far the tentative accord between Mick and Davies might have gone had not the tramp overplayed his hand and presumed upon his superior. It is possible to envision Aston becoming a tramp, supplanted by the vicious alliance of Mick and Davies. One need recall only Flora and Barnabas to see how tempting to Pinter that twist might have been.

Again the vehicle through which the values of the play are made manifest is language. Robert Brustein charges in *Seasons of Discontent* that Pinter refuses to communicate in *The Caretaker*, that the "language, while authentic colloquial speech, is stripped bare of reflective or conceptual thought, so that the play could be just as effectively performed in Finno-Ugric. You might say that *The Caretaker* approaches the condition of music—if you could conceive of music without much development, lyric quality, or thematic content." [10] One wonders if all philosophy must be "philosophical" or theology "theological." Must language communicate only by "saying something"? Brustein criticizes the conceiver for not being conceptual on the one hand and on the other attacks imaginary creations for being too concrete. Furthermore, we are told, *The Caretaker* approaches the condition of music.[11] How could the critic bestow a greater benediction? Apparently the gulf between the insight of Pater and that of some modern critics is larger than one suspects. The language of *The Caretaker*, in its halts, its pauses, its measured cadences does approach the condition of music. In a discussion about the filming of *The Caretaker*, Pinter expressly noted how sensitive he was to "The balance, the timing, and the rhythm to this, the silent music, as it were. . . ." [12]

The real charge that Brustein and other advocates of "the committed theatre" seem to be making is that Pinter refuses to provide a rallying cry, a call to arms for one cause or another. Pinter simply goes about doing whatever it is that he does and thereby makes it difficult for critics to appropriate him for their categories. Pinter has tried to do the most difficult of things, to talk about whatever it is we cannot talk about and for his effort, he is told that he lacks thematic content. Pinter gives voice to the silences, something poets have tried to do since Orpheus, and he is told that there is no lyricism in the proletarian paeans of Davies, Mick, and Aston.

The difficult trick which Pinter tries to turn in *The Caretaker* is to show the way in which the language succeeds in revealing most profoundly by seeming to fail. Pinter started with the most mundane situation.

> It seemed to me that when you have two people standing on the stairs and one asks the other if he would like to be caretaker in the house, and the other bloke, you know, who is work-shy, doesn't want in fact to say no, he doesn't want the job, but at the same time he wants to edge it around.[13]

It is in the "edging around" that the real conflicts of the play emerge. To Davies, for example, the passivity of Aston is like speaking to a blank wall. All he gets back is the garbled echo of his own speech and he becomes thereby even more radically isolated.

There are other ways in which Pinter communicates by seeming not to communicate. The recurrent references to the Buddha statuette provide one example. The real symbols of the play, the shoes, the shed, et. al. are so mundane that one naturally expects the Buddha to function symbolically as well; but it does not. One could see it as the ordered center of a disordered universe but that takes us nowhere. One could see it as the omphalos, the cynosure of the character's hopes and aspirations, but the characters really do not seem to mind that much about it. Or consider the incessant leak in the ceiling which drips into the bucket. When Davies asks what they do when the bucket is full, Aston replies that they empty it. The potential symbol is likewise emptied. Dukore notes further the many "symbols of non-connection."[14] Aston cannot fix the electric plug, for example. But these images do not seem to lead anywhere either. The point behind all of these non-symbols is that the symbols, the referents, the guidelines are not functioning. Davies wants to make his way in the world, to make the "right connections"; and he seeks the deeper explanation behind the phenomenal appearances, but there is none.

The assignment Pinter gives himself is to make it possible for a character like Davies to stumble, pause, repeat himself, and blunder into confused silence and still be able to communicate himself to us. Pinter has confessed, "I am pretty well obsessed with words when they get going. It is a matter of tying the words to the image of the character standing on the stage. The two things go very closely together." [15] It is in the sundry recitals of silence, then, that Pinter's recurrent themes are integrated and articulated. Pinter had originally thought *The Caretaker* should end in violence, probably in the death of Davies.[16] But as he reconsidered the conclusion, he decided that the characters as he had set them in motion would not have resorted to violence. Violence, Pinter notes, is just one of the special strategies by which people compete for dominance. The struggle for dominance had resolved itself as a linguistic struggle in which Davies could not finally compete. Mick was quick to point out to the tramp that he rather easily got out of his depth, that he could not finally win the language game.

It is easy to feel out of one's depth with the plays of Pinter. One always faces the question "what is this about?" or "what is he doing?" Amend, for one, argues that Pinter and Brecht are alike in their use of the "V-effect" (*Verfremdungseffekt*). "Like Brecht, Pinter seeks to alienate, or distance, his characters from the spectator in order that the spectator will become involved rationally in what is happening on stage." [17] When Pinter's drama is at its best, it is true that the audience may wish to evaluate what is going on; but their involvement is not so much rational as non-rational. Insofar as the nameless anxieties that haunt the characters are validly, that is to say dramatically, rendered, the observer is drawn into the same circle of anxiety. We are not all itinerant caretakers, of course; but we are all, in our own way, care-taken wanderers. If we rationalize while watching Pinter's plays, it is more likely that we are trying to hypostatize into categories the encircling metaphors of the play, to beat off their seductive gestures with our reasoned principles.

We may best permit *The Caretaker* to function if we resist localizing it or allegorizing it. After the commercial failure of *The Birthday Party*, Pinter lived in a basement and worked as a caretaker for some time in London's Notting Hill district. Davies is drawn from a composite of all the tramps he saw although one in particular continued to return to his mind.[18] *The Caretaker* may not have been written if Pinter had not had those particular experiences in Notting Hill. But in no way does the success of *The Caretaker* in speaking to many who have never seen a basement in Notting Hill depend on the author's experiences.

Similarly, no allegory will serve the cause of understanding *The Caretaker*. Arnold Hinchliffe records a conversation between Pinter and playwright Terence Rattigan about *The Caretaker*.[19] Rattigan observed, "When I saw *The Caretaker*, I told Pinter that I knew what it meant, 'It's about the God of the Old Testament, the God of the New, and Humanity, isn't it?' " Pinter replied, "No, Terry, it's about a caretaker and two brothers." Pinter's response is, of course, more of his dissimulation; but it is also the only kind of response any playwright ought to make. Like any good poet, Pinter refuses to cut off the possibilities of his metaphors, refuses to make it possible for us to deny their radical applicability. *The Caretaker*, finally, is about a caretaker and two brothers. It's about this chap who 'as to get to Sidcup. . . . 'e's got 'is papers there. . . . We ought to be able to see . . . simplicity of the thing is so . . . have to get down to Sidcup ourselves one of these days . . . weather will be clearing shortly and . . . but you get the drift. . . .

4

The Homecoming

In his essay "Remembrance of the Poet," Martin Heidegger concludes, "all the poems of the poet who has entered into his poethood are poems of homecoming." Pinter's two act play *The Homecoming* (1965), reveals an assured craftsman who knows what he wants to do and is doing it. For many *The Homecoming* is not as satisfying a play as *The Care-taker*,[1] but there is little doubt that *The Homecoming* is a rich fusion of the previous themes of the search for a secure home, the poverty of the self, and the struggle for possession. In his first "Duino Elegy," Rilke asks us to "notice that we're not very much at home in the world we've expounded." The possibilities of homecoming in our time, of "the return into the proximity of the source" to continue Heidegger's analysis, is not a facile accomplishment. Home, the abiding place of the self, the place where we really live is that which is most difficult to recover.

The Homecoming trades on the conventional plot of a young man who brings his bride home to meet the folks. From that point on, the convention is discarded for a parlor game as terrifying and corrosive as Stanley's birthday party. Teddy, the young man, brings his wife Ruth back to his family home in England. Teddy is a philosophy professor in the United States and has not seen his family for six years; and they have never met his new wife. The head of the household is Max, a seventy-year-old butcher. His wife Jessie has been dead a number of years, leaving behind two other sons besides Teddy—Lenny, a panderer, and Joey, a demolition expert by day and a boxer by night. One other character, Sam, the slightly younger brother of Max, completes the loving family circle.

Max is the primal father, compassionate provider and *pater tyrannus* in one. He constantly seeks devotion from his sons and yet continues to assert his autocratic authority. In the initial scene, for example, Max makes continued demands on Lenny, to pass him the scissors, to give him a cigarette when he already has a cigarette in his pocket. Lenny's only response is to suggest that his father is demented. Max thinks back on the time when he and his friend MacGregor were the terrors of the West End. His remembrance of strength past only sharpens Lenny's insolence, and he warns his son that he will "chop your spine off, you talk to me like that!" (9). Max's choice of imagery seems appropriate for a professional butcher. But it is apparent even in the first scene that the family circle seethes with suppressed hostility. The games the father and sons play seem to have too much zest to be wholly innocent. But perhaps the most chilling game of all is the way they play at being a family. In mock filial piety Lenny bows before his father and pleads with "Daddy" not to beat his little boy.

Sam then replaces Lenny in confronting Max. Sam describes his day as a chauffeur; he is the best man in the company because first, he is a good driver and second, he does not take liberties with the passengers. Max deflates Sam by asking him why he never got married, whether it was true or not that he is not "above having a good bang on the back seat" (15). Sam replies that he leaves that sort of thing to others, a hint which he will later clarify. In still another ironic adumbration, Max tells his brother that if and when he does get married, he can bring his bride home and she can keep them all happy.

The third son Joey enters and asks for a meal. Max lashes back.

> Who do you think I am, your mother? Eh? Honest. They walk in here every time of the day and night like bloody animals. Go and find yourself a mother. (16)

In his denunciation Max articulates two of the compelling images of the play. The number of animal images in the play suggests the visceral level at which the characters live. Max is a butcher who spends his time talking about the horses at Epsom Downs. He compares his sons to animals and even tries to carve them up as a butcher would. Later he says of Ruth that she will turn them all into animals. Lenny replies that his father's cooking is fit for dogs. But in the presence of this animal imagery, Max introduces the more important theme of the play—the search for a mother. When Ruth enters the scene, she merges these themes and brings out the animal instincts of the men and the homecoming takes on the air of a prenuptial rite.

After the family has gone to bed for the night, Teddy arrives with his wife. He shows Ruth about the living room and explains how a wall was moved.

> We knocked it down . . . years ago . . . to make an open living area. The structure wasn't affected, you see. My mother was dead. (21)

The structure of the room was not affected, but his implicit confession makes it clear that the structure of the family was profoundly affected. Ruth does not seem eager to stay and wonders whether the children back in the United States are missing them. Teddy reminds her that they will just be visiting for a short while and that he wants very much for her to meet his family. "They're very warm people, really. Very warm. They're my family. They're not ogres" (23). A basic pattern of disagreement is established between Teddy and Ruth. They are not quarreling overtly; but they progressively find themselves on the opposing sides of questions that are ultimately transformed into crucial differences.

While Ruth goes out for a walk, Lenny wanders in and greets Teddy with a casualness that belies their long separation. Lenny explains that he has not been sleeping well of late.

LENNY   No, I wouldn't say I was dreaming. It's not exactly a dream. It's just that something keeps waking me up. Some kind of tick.

TEDDY   A tick?

LENNY   Yes.

TEDDY   Well, what is it?

LENNY   I don't know.
[*pause*]
TEDDY   Have you got a clock in your room?
LENNY   Yes.
TEDDY   Well, maybe it's the clock.
LENNY   Yes, could be, I suppose.
[*pause*]
Well, if it's the clock I'd better do something about it.
Stifle it in some way, or something. (25)

The skillful exploitation of the pauses, the weighted reference to the "tick," reveal Pinter's capacity once again to
invest the ordinary with the sense of menace. The tick
becomes a metonymy for the general malaise that the family
and especially Lenny feels. Properly delivered, the speech
takes on a gravity that is easy to miss in reading. Properly
delivered, the speech hangs in the silence and accretes the
collective tick of time that one hears only in the deepest
night.

Lenny stays up after Ted goes to bed and thus meets Ruth
when she returns from her walk. He asks her if she is
connected with his brother in some way, and Ruth replies
that they are married. Without pausing, Lenny ignores her
reply and asks her advice about the tick that troubles him.
He explains that he is not at all sure that it was the clock,
that there are all sorts of things that look proper during the
day but "let out a bit of a tick" or two at night. Things are
deceptive he explains. He asks her again whether she lives
with Teddy in America. He refuses to accept the legality of
her relationship; he refuses to conclude that things are always what they appear to be.

Lenny asks to hold her hand, offering to explain but he
does not. He tries to take a glass of water from Ruth, but she
refuses to relinquish it. The test of wills between the two has
emerged silently between Lenny's rambling anecdotes and
seemingly unrelated observations. Ruth calls him "Leonard"
and thereby seems to attain the authority over the "Other"
for which they are contending. He pleads with her not to call
him Leonard because that was the name his mother gave
him. Ruth tells him that if he takes the glass, she will take

him. He accuses her of visiting in order to start trouble; and Ruth offers him the glass in a scene which suggests a partly erotic, partly maternal relationship emerging between the two. Ruth seems capable of defending herself in this den of "animals" and seems to know how to establish her dominance by tacitly assuming the dual role of mother and temptress.

Lenny's dalliance with Ruth reveals him in turn to be erotic but impotent. As a procurer, he leads a vicarious existence, feeding on the vitality of others. Ruth tumbles to his game and offers him a combination of herself and water, a psychological amalgam of the erotic and maternal elements.

Since the death of Jessie, the family circle has been incomplete. The mother-mistress is missing. Max has accordingly had to assume the role of the missing female. He cooks for the family, even says he likes the kitchen and hates the living room. (Perhaps he hates the living room because Jessie's chair in the family circle remains empty.) Max further claims to feel the birth pangs sustained while bringing his three sons into the world. While Max has assumed the maternal as well as the paternal role, it is clear that he does not like playing Mum for a group of boys with healthy glands.

Teddy and Ruth get up late the next morning, and Max is infuriated to learn that he was not informed of their arrival. He asks Teddy who the slut is he has with him. He ignores Teddy's hesitant attempts to explain that Ruth is his wife and declares to Teddy "I've never had a whore under this roof before. Ever since your mother died. My word of honour" (42). His reminder can, of course, be taken two ways. Only when he learns that Ruth is the mother of three children does he warm to her. Only when the maternal side of Ruth is underlined does Max welcome her into the family. He then asks Teddy to "have a cuddle" with him, concluding the first act with the observation that Teddy still loves his father. Teddy and Max are really squaring off in their reunion although it is apparent that Teddy is still subservient to his domineering father. Teddy is being welcomed not so much because he has returned home but because he has brought Ruth with him. Max explained while talking about horses that he could always look a filly in the eye "and by the look deep down in her eye I could tell whether she was a stayer or not" (10). Max has apparently liked what he has seen in the depths of Ruth's eyes. She is, apparently, "a stayer."

The second act begins with Ruth sitting in the chair vacated by Jessie and surrounded by her new family. Seeing Ruth there stirs Max to recall previous family gatherings. He wishes that Jessie were alive and then he explains to Ruth that Jessie taught the boys all the morality they know. She was, he adds, the backbone of the family. But when he thinks of the way in which some of his dreams turned sour, he immediately changes tone and denounces his "crippled family, three bastard sons, a slutbitch of a wife. . . ." (47). The strong emotional ambivalence which each member of the family seems to harbor emerges with astonishing rapidity and suddenness. Just as suddenly he gives his blessing to Teddy and Ruth.

Teddy seems unnerved by the way in which Ruth has been taken to the bosom of the family. He tries to justify himself, to bolster his ego; and without overt reference, he reminds Ruth of their life in the United States.

TEDDY   She's a great help to me over there. She's a wonderful wife and mother. She's a very popular woman. She's got lots of friends. It's a great life, at the University . . . you know . . . it's a very good life. We've got a lovely house . . . we've got all . . . we've got everything we want. It's a very stimulating environment.
[*pause*]
My department . . . is highly successful.
[*pause*]
We've got three boys, you know. (50)

Ted's halting delivery is reminiscent of Davies, and one suspects the same kind of uncertainty and lack of confidence lies behind the rhetoric. When Max, after surveying his family, asks Ruth, "tell me, do you think the children are missing their mother," Teddy misunderstands which family

Max is alluding to and replies, "Of course they are. They love her. We'll be seeing them soon" (51). In the pause that follows, Lenny observes that Ted's cigar has gone out. Thus by way of the awkward silences, the misunderstandings, and the reference to external objects like the burnt out cigar, Pinter conveys the emptiness of Teddy and the life which he offers Ruth.

The emptiness of Teddy becomes further apparent under cross-examination by Lenny. When Lenny asks the Doctor of Philosophy about the central affirmations of Christian theism, questions of significance for any serious philosopher, Teddy replies that the matter does not fall within his province. When Lenny asks how they are to regard a table, for example, the responses seem consistent with their general personalities. Teddy thinks that the table is finally a table; Max says Lenny, the procurer, would sell it; and Joey, the boxer and demolition man, says he would chop it up for firewood. But Ruth brings the disquisition to a halt by observing,

> Don't be too sure though. You've forgotten something. Look at me. I . . . move my leg. That's all it is. But I wear . . . underwear . . . which moves with me . . . it . . . captures your attention. Perhaps you misinterpret. The action is simple. It's a leg . . . moving. My lips move. Why don't you restrict . . . your observations to that? Perhaps the fact that they move is more significant . . . than the words which come through them. You must bear that . . . possibility . . . in mind. (52, 53)

Ruth again substitutes her intense physical presence, her concrete reality and reduces all philosophy to idle and irrelevant speculation. She is also urging everyone to be aware of the difference between what seems and what is, between appearance and reality. Her speech echoes Lenny's earlier (28) comment that things at night look different than during the day. Furthermore, she seems to be describing Pinter's own technique. The fact that something is being said or is not being said is ultimately more important (because more revealing) than what it is that is being said. Ruth's presence, then, continues to dominate. She becomes the center of their collective consciousness.

While Teddy has gone to pack their bags, Ruth explains to Lenny that before she got married, she was a model. Her euphemism becomes clearer when she dances seductively with Lenny and reveals that she is embarked on a second round of her homecoming, the return to her original vocation after a six-year sabbatical in the United States. Lenny and Joey hover about Ruth kissing her while Max tells Teddy that he is happy that his son has brought such a fine woman home. Ruth gets up from her embrace and begins ordering the men around; she is now at the center of power in the household as well as the center of their collective consciousness.

As Ruth sits at the center of the room, Teddy reminds his family that they would not understand his critical treatises. Teddy's defense of his work is obviously a defense of his own potency and right to Ruth.

> You'd be lost. It's nothing to do with the question of in-
> telligence. It's a way of being able to look at the world.
> It's a question of how far you can operate on things and
> not in things. I mean it's a question of your capacity to
> ally the two, to relate the two, to balance the two. To see,
> to be able to SEE! I'm the one who can see. That's why
> I can write my critical works. Might do you good . . .
> have a look at them . . . see how certain people can view
> . . . things . . . how certain people can maintain . . .
> intellectual equilibrium. Intellectual equilibrium. You're
> just objects. You just . . . move about. I can observe it.
> I can see what you do. It's the same as I do. But you're
> lost in it. You won't get me being . . . I won't be lost
> in it. (61, 62)

Teddy's works are strictly analytic and non-procreative. It is clear that the mood and method of his work is to avoid involvement in the subjective world. He prefers to be objective in a world of objects and his rational system has no place for the chthonic forces that move his family. Teddy reproaches the others for being lost in the world, and he fails to realize that he also will be lost precisely because he cannot lose himself in the real world. The lacunae in Teddy's rhetorical facade thus originate in the emptiness that is his center.

The play concludes with Teddy returning to the United States without Ruth. Ruth has agreed to stay with Max and his boys, and they have agreed to set her up in business as a part-time prostitute. Teddy has gone and Sam has collapsed in dismay. Max wonders if she will not in fact be using them rather than the reverse. His suspicion is reinforced by the denouement which finds Ruth at the center of the stage, obviously in command, with Joey and Lenny and Max clinging to her. The scene is a parody of the family portrait; mother has come home.

A more detailed consideration of the characters of *The Homecoming* elicits some of the deeper patterns of the play. Why, for example, does Teddy leave Ruth and return to the United States without his wife and the mother of his children? One can only speculate, for Pinter characteristically does not elaborate. Perhaps Teddy hopes that Ruth will follow once she realizes the implications of the homecoming; but Ruth does seem to realize and to accept the conditions of her exchange, and he has thus grossly miscalculated. As the eldest son, the Oedipal burden falls upon Teddy most heavily; and yet he seems the most incapable of standing up to his father and to his family. Perhaps he hopes that Ruth will have the strength to resist where he did not. Initially Ruth wanted to get back to the United States, perhaps because of her recognition of her own temptation. Yet this explanation does not satisfy, for Ruth possesses a great deal of strength although not a strength that is likely to be employed on behalf of her weak husband.

In many respects Teddy is the most chilling character in the play. His emotional detachment permits him to play the game according to the lines of power. He does not have the power to control Ruth and thus willingly gives her up, willingly plays the family game. But, finally, one analysis seems most consistent with the text. Teddy cannot contend with his family because he is impotent as a human being. Teddy is given to philosophical abstractions and is incapable of dealing with the concrete presence of Ruth and his family.

His inability to alter the fate of Ruth and Sam forces him to participate in the brutality of his family, not out of conviction but out of weakness. Behind the cultured facade, Teddy is hollow and the hollow man has no business in the arena with the animals. Teddy considers the odds and prudently retires from the field. He returns to the United States to be the mother to his three children. He has become, like Davies, the outsider who has been vanquished. Again, those in the room have won. Of Teddy, it could finally be observed as in the conclusion to Matthias Claudius' poem "Man,"

> *Denn legt er sich zu seinen Vätern nieder,*
> *Und er kömmt nimmer wieder.*
> (He lays himself where his fathers laid before
> And returns home nevermore).

Sam is perhaps the only sympathetic character in *The Homecoming*. He reveals in the silences of his speech that he too loved Jessie and perhaps would have treated her a bit better than Max. He has, however, had to stand on the sidelines all of his life and watch others. Now, in the return of Ruth, he sees the cycle beginning again. The rightful husband is being supplanted. He protests the arrangement, saying that there are legal ties between Teddy and Ruth even though the family has consistently seemed uninterested in the legality of the relationship. One suspects that Sam's protest is not only a deontological argument but an anthropological plea. He wants to save and respect the institution of marriage in order to save man from himself. His dilemma is to find himself in a group that obeys the laws of the blood, laws which are preconscious, presocietal.

Finally in his desperation, Sam screams "MacGregor had Jessie in the back of my cab as I drove them along" (78). Then he collapses on the floor. Sam cannot cope with the den of animals either. Teddy lacks the moral courage to oppose his family, and Sam lacks the physical strength. His collapse is his particular means of exiting from an untenable situation.

Sam and Max perhaps comprise the composite father. The antitheses of provider-tyrant, lover-mate, respecter of womanhood-seducer seem to be personified in Sam and Max respectively. (Both are, of course, sons of the same father.) Max's sons, Lenny and Joey, similarly seem to be aberrations, to be partial men. In the final tableau, Lenny stands watching while Joey rests his head in Ruth's lap. Lenny, the panderer, is still hovering over the lovers, still outside, still participating in life vicariously. Joey remains a brute who is without intellectual capabilities but nonetheless suited for the violent game that has transpired. They are all, then, truncated human beings in search of completion.

Perhaps the second most important character in the play does not appear; she is the missing Jessie. Jessie's death created a vacuum in the family and accordingly the men have had to substitute for the missing feminine. Max does all the cooking, talks about his pangs of childbirth, and calls his sons "bitches." When Teddy's family loses its woman in turn, Teddy will have to take over the wifely duties. What kind of person Jessie was seems clear enough. Max observes that Jessie taught the boys all the morality they know. He calls her "a slut-bitch" even as he confesses his love for her. Sam further revealed that she had been in the back seat with MacGregor, and one suspects that one or more of Max's sons were fathered by MacGregor. Thus Ted's return with Ruth, wife, mother of three sons, and part-time whore, seems to provide a fitting surrogate for the missing Jessie.

Ruth is clearly the nexus of *The Homecoming*. She is wife, mother, daughter-in-law, sister-in-law, whore, and eternal feminine. She is all things to all people. She is the point of origin and return, the locus of the coming home. Her circumference is nowhere and her center is everywhere. Pascal, echoing Bruno and de Lille, once noted, "nature is an infinite sphere whose center is everywhere, whose circumference is nowhere." Ruth is the natural end, the uroboros, the omphalos, the world navel and vortex of all beginnings. The homecoming is the coming home of Ruth, and those who come to Ruth have come home. In *The Room* Rose is asked to go home with Riley but cannot because of her weakness; in *The Homecoming* Ruth is asked to go home with Teddy but will not because she is already home. The words of the biblical Ruth have returned upon the house of Teddy, for Ruth has made his people her people.

The fecundity of Pinter challenges the ingenuity of the critics, and the critics have had a good time with *The Homecoming*. One interpretation, perhaps the silliest, sees Teddy as Harold Pinter who, in 1965, was presenting his work (Ruth) to his family (the public) after an absence from the stage of six years.[2] This is obviously a point of view that one would not wish to push very far. Theological allegories make little sense either. One commentator sees Max and his family as Beelzebub and his company of demons. Ted equals the evil of intelligence, Lenny the evil of flesh, and Joey the evil of brute force.[3] A psychiatrist sees *The Homecoming* as an extension of the *ménage à trois* prefigured in *The Collection*. All of the men in the household hate women in their individual ways and profane the air with their degrading opinions of women. Behind all this malevolence, of course, is a homosexual association which is dominated by Max in his role as cook, maid, and Mum for the household. When confronted by a woman, they are powerless; they succumb to heart attacks, impotence, or childlike dependence. The subsequent *ménage à cinq* provides the occasion for the vicarious enjoyment of each other through overt heterosexual behavior.[4] All of these interpretations are tidy but seem to leave a number of unanswered questions.

Still another critic has called *The Homecoming* "a comedy of manners"[5] because, primarily, it is concerned with social rather than psychological behavior. There is much to recommend a sociological approach to *The Homecoming*. While the characters seem to be individuals, they are also part of a social unit, a tribal family as it were. As Lenny explains to the recalcitrant Teddy, "we do make up a unit, Teddy, and you're an integral part of it. When we all sit round the backyard having a quiet gander at the night sky, there's always an empty chair standing in the circle, which is in fact yours" (65). One does not have to push his imagination too far to see a circle of primitives sitting beneath the sky in silence.[6]

Though they are individuals living in separate rooms, the

characters emerge from their cells to congregate as a family in the large living room, the clearing in the wilderness. Since the mother's death, the living room has been enlarged; if the room were still small, they would tear each other to pieces. As Max says with typical paternal devotion, "I'll chop your spine off." If the family is a tribe then, their language is appropriately a series of grunts and grimaces, promises and threats to wheedle or terrify others into compliance.

Although *The Homecoming* is more than a social drama, a comedy of manners, the "homecoming" has been interpreted in four sociological ways—Jessie (in the person of Ruth) returns to her home; Ruth as mother brings a sense of home back to the family; Ruth has come to her new home and Ted to his old; and Ruth's entrance restores potency to the household.[7]

Critic John Warner has argued that *The Homecoming* is a dramatization of the plight of contemporary man in the time of the eclipsed gods and their sorry substitutes, Science and Rationalism. Consciously or unconsciously, then, the characters of the play represent their fellows in a search for psychic wholeness. When, for example, Lenny pins his hopes on Second Wind at Sandown Park (9), he testifies to his unspoken need for renewal, for a new wind to blow through the wasteland. (The etymological relationship of wind and spirit, respiration and inspiration, *ésprit* and *spiritus* reinforces Warner's contention.) Lenny's deepest gesture, then, is to find the right nag on which to ride home a winner.[8] But we have seen before that the most mundane situations which Pinter has conjured up have been capable of speaking to the depths of our collective psyche. *The Homecoming,* thus, is finally about the business of coming home.

The business of coming home is part of the collective, that is, archetypal experience of man. The separate characters of *The Homecoming* comprise a single person. Max is the hunter, the butcher, the provider; Lenny the arranger, the go-between, the social man; Joey, the violent man, the protector; Teddy, the intellectual, the thinking man; Sam, the feeling man. Together they are a composite man in search of the composite woman—Ruth—who is the eternal feminine, wife, mother, and enchantress. Together this sextet could make beautiful music, but they are not quite able to effect the union.

The arena of the play may be social, the relationships psychological, but the deepest currents in the play are archetypal. In Heideggerian terms the collective man is trying to attain the collective woman, to come "in proximity to the source." The union, the "happy marriage" of the alchemists, is the unification of the antitheses of the human consciousness, the recovery of the uroboros, the re-cognition of paradise, the homecoming. Several other Pinter plays have dramatized the multivalent nature of the female as mother, lover and a host of other associations in Rose, Meg, Flora, and Sarah. All of these associations are combined in Pinter's characterization of Ruth and her boys.

In the original version of the speech cited above, Lenny explained Teddy's participation in the family in somewhat more explicit terms.

> We may be a little dull, but we still have an eye for mother nature, and often in fact sit out in the back yard having a quiet gander at the night sky. Our little community, our quiet little group, our team, you might say, our unit, made up of, I'll admit it, various and not entirely similar component parts, but which, put together, do nevertheless make up a whole. An organism, which, though we're not exactly a sentimental family, we do recognize as such. And you're an integral part of it, Ted.[9]

What the collective man of *The Homecoming* is trying to do is to unite with the source, the source which is often personified in erotic and maternal imagery. Perhaps it is because they have long been in search of each other that Ruth and the men of the family seem to know each other, seem to accept each other's presence. The unspoken gestures of the play do not imply ignorance so much as recognition of that which lies beyond language. The final tableau is a dramatization of silence. Ted's protests have been stilled; Sam lies prostrate on the floor; Lenny, Joey, and Max are almost literally bowing before the seated Ruth. Their silence is a sign of recognition, a token of homage not so much to Ruth as to the train of collective associations which she carries behind her. The silence of the conclusion is the silence of kenosis wherein each of the characters has emptied himself in order to become fuller. Each of the characters, together the composite man, participates in something larger than the self. Each participates in the archetype of original unity, the return to the source, the homecoming.[10] In 1800 Hölderlin described the process of archetypal attainment which transpires in the linguistic lacunae of *The Homecoming*.

. . . therefore has language, most dangerous of possessions, been given to man, so that creating, destroying, and perishing and returning to the ever-living, to the mistress and mother, he may affirm what he is.

The issue of morality has often been raised in connection with *The Homecoming*. At the superficial level, *The Homecoming* is a shocking play, an affront even to the morality of those who live in a morally fluid age. But the characters of *The Homecoming* are no more concerned with moral issues than a dog is self-conscious about his relationship to a fire hydrant. That is not to dismiss the characters as being merely animals. Rather they are dramatizations of a region of the human consciousness which lies below volition and is amoral in character. When asked if *The Homecoming* represented a descent into pure evil, Pinter replied, "There is no question that the family does behave very calculatedly and pretty horribly to each other and to the returning son. But they do it out of the texture of their lives and for other reasons which are not evil but slightly desperate." [11] Elsewhere in the interview, he notes that the characters act the way they do not "arbitrarily but for very deep-seated reasons." The "deep-seated reasons" are part of that human experience which lies beyond good and evil. They, like those who went before and like those who shall follow, are about the business of coming home, the return to the proximity of the source.

Where will Pinter go after he has gone home? Where can one go who gropes for the unseen, who seeks to give voice to the unspeakable? *The Homecoming* suggests the possibility that his silences are widening and are extending themselves toward the expression of compelling human archetypes. For all their refusal to leave "this world," Pinter's characters nevertheless strain for something beyond. The transcendental motive need not take its grounding in a specifically theological, philosophical, or cultural pattern to be authentic. Lenny tells us in *The Homecoming* that neither the known nor the unknown merits our reverence. But the silence which ensues from such a confession need not necessarily be arid. Neither is it necessary to conclude that to arrive home is to have completed one's venture. If the Pinter corpus can develop beyond *The Homecoming*, if the ensuing forms continue to be "original," if the silences continue to be procreative, then he will have demonstrated that "the way home is the way forward." [12]

5

The Rest Is Silence
Silence, Landscape

In an interview with critic Judith Crist that appeared in *Look*, December 24, 1968, Harold Pinter observed,

> It's a little fatiguing when people talk about my damn pauses.
> . . . It becomes metaphysical. Actually, I write the pause because people are going to stop talking at this point.

Six months later London's Royal Shakespeare Company premiered his most recent work, two one-act plays titled *Landscape* and *Silence*. The silences are there. They are integral to the efficacy of Pinter's theatre. And the student of Pinter must come to terms with them.

The movement toward *Landscape*, the silences rendered pictorial, and toward *Silence*, the linguistic assemblage of silence, was implicit in the beginning. The silences of the last plays differ only in degree, not in kind from the silence which surrounded Rose, the Birthday Boy, and Davies. Throughout the corpus, characters try and ostensibly fail in their efforts to fling linguistic bridges across the abyss. But the abyss widens or deepens and the ballistic potential of their language is again outdistanced. Thus, the silence deepens. Samuel Beckett manifested a similar movement in the unfolding of his corpus. Given the isolation of his characters, given their exhaustion and immobility, he found it judicious in *Play* to place them in large urns. Those urns became thus the literalization of their a priori conditions. From those encapsulated environments, the characters could touch each other neither by hand nor movement of spirit. They were, in short, alone as they had always been alone. Similarly, Pinter has pushed his latest incarnations of Rose and the Birthday Boy and Davies to the literalization of their condition.

While the early characters moved in a generally realistic environment, however strange and unreal that environment often seemed, the last characters do not move about very much at all. Their isolation is intensified, literalized; their movements and gestures toward each other are mechanical and rigid. Their discouse is more fragmentary than before. They begin somewhere near where Davies ended. Their conversation proceeds at different levels and rarely is there a point of intersection. Each seems caught in the prison of himself, in the strictures of an unrelieved past, and blessed (or cursed) with only a partial insight into the nature of his condition.

The plays that Pinter has written have always been short, tightly constructed pieces, even plays like *The Caretaker* in which a great deal of circumlocution and meandering was necessary to make a certain point. Concision is always an aesthetic virtue. However, the poet runs the risk of saying nothing as he increasingly moves toward the Word which lies behind all other words, the secret syllable, the talismanic name of the god in hiding. He may, if the process continues, if he lives long enough, if he has the courage to follow whither his vision leads him, come at last to speak the cosmic OM or its equivalent or speak nothing at all. Such will not be drama, however. Drama demands some kind of action even if the specific action is the action of non-action as in *Play*. When in *The Poetics* Aristotle argued for a unity of action, it is clear from the context that he intended a unity of motive, a vision of a whole which could hold the separate movements together.[1] Thus Shakespeare in *King Lear* does not in any sense violate the unity of the play's action by unfolding both the Lear-Cordelia plot line and the Glouces-ter-Edmund plot line, both testifying to a father undone by his offspring and, further, implicated in his own undoing. While no one particularly cares what notions Shakespeare violated on his way to the stage, the fact remains that OM or its equivalent will not make a play. As Pinter follows the direction of his vision, as he moves ever toward the OM, he runs the risk of replacing drama with apotheosis, of trading the stage for the temple.

A superficial response to *Landscape* and to *Silence* might

conclude that Pinter has indeed left drama somewhere behind for the recesses of a vision so private, so arcane as to be
incommunicable and even uninteresting to others. *Time*
magazine loftily adopts such a view. The anonymous reviewer inverts the dictum of Mies van der Rohe that "less is
more" by concluding of Pinter's development that "less is
less." *Landscape* and *Silence* are skillful games in which we
get the point but nothing else, the reviewer concludes. The
same argument has been heard with every one of the earlier
plays with the exception of *The Homecoming* in which there
was even some question as to the point. The question, then,
seems whether Pinter has at last crossed that fine line between drama dramatized and drama interiorized to the point
of eclipse.

In *Silence* (1969), the first play on the twin bill, though the
last to be published, three characters—Ellen, a girl in her
twenties, Rumsey, a man of forty, and Bates, a man in his
mid-thirties—are positioned in three separate areas of the
stage equally appointed with chair, bed, and table. In any
such dramatic situation or set of givens, only so many alter-
natives are possible. The three may live cosily together in a
highly civilized *ménage à trois*, any two may pair off to the
exclusion of the third, or the three may remain isolated from
each other. Pinter raises the first two options as possibilities
and considers their failure from the vantage point of the
third, the condition of isolation. Within the condition of
isolation a number of options are open. The characters may
strive to overcome their isolation and effect some relationship with each other. They may remain content with their
isolation either because they prefer it or because they are
ignorant of other options. Or they may accept the essential
isolation of their condition and yet remain aware in some
way of the other options as unrealized in the past and most
likely unrealizable in the future. In *Silence* Pinter raises all of
these possibilities and does not decide between them. The
characters are forever in the realm of the fragmentary, the
hypothetical, the provisional. Perhaps they had a relationship

once. Perhaps a relationship is possible in the future. In any case, the present is composed of an illusive and allusive phantasmagoria of bits and pieces suggesting a whole fabric but never displaying it.

Rumsey, for example, speaks of walking with a girl in gray who holds his arm, while about them a dog barks and the moon slips between the clouds. Ellen observes,

> There are two. One who is with me sometimes, and another. He listens to me. I tell him what I know. We walk by the dogs. Sometimes the wind is so high he does not hear me. I lead him to a tree, clasp closely to him and whisper to him, wind going, dogs stop, and he hears me.
> But the other hears me. (2)

The ostensible similarity of their descriptions suggests that Ellen and Rumsey and Ellen and Bates are the people involved. But the logical connections, the sequential pattern does not emerge and so we are left without verification, a familiar experience for the Pinter audience.

Bates, for example, observes,

> It's a question of sleep. I need something of it, or how can I remain alive, without any true rest, having no solace, no constant solace, not even any damn inconstant solace.
> I am strong, but not as strong as the bastards in the other room, and their tittering bitches, and their music, and their love.
> If I changed my life, perhaps, and lived deliberately at night, and slept in the day. But what exactly would I do? What can be meant by living in the dark? (4)

What can be meant by living in the dark is the metaphysical question that characterizes the entire play, even, the entire Pinter corpus. If we changed our lives and lived deliberately in the face of darkness, what exactly would we do; what would be the consequences, the hopes entertained? Bates may be raising the right question after all and, however uncertain the answer, raising the right kind of question may well be better than not knowing what the question is.

There are a few pivotal points in the play, a few abortive

movements out of isolation. Bates moves over toward Ellen and asks, "Will we meet tonight?" "I don't know," she replies. "*Pause*" (6). Such is the question, such the answer. As the protagonist of T. S. Eliot's "Gerontion" observes,

> I would meet you upon this honestly.
> I that was near your heart was removed therefrom
> To lose beauty in terror, terror in inquisition.
> I have lost my passion: why should I need to keep it
> Since what is kept must be adulterated?
> I have lost my sight, smell, hearing, taste and touch:
> How should I use them for your closer contact?

The specific etiology leading to the space between Ellen and Bates may vary from that between Gerontion and whomever he would meet. The degree of self-insight certainly varies. But Ellen's "I don't know" how it is that we are to meet differs in degree though not in kind from Gerontion's estrangement. Ellen does know that she wants to go somewhere else (7), to go where she is not now. When asked where, she cannot say. She knows that she does not wish to be where she is now, to have the range of possibilities open to her so severely limited, but she cannot say where it is that she must go in order to be where she *is*. She cannot, in short, effect the homecoming that lies at the end of all departures.

Rumsey reinforces the disquieted isolation of Ellen by observing that,

> Sometimes I see people. They walk towards me, no, not so, walk in my direction, but never reaching me, turning left, or disappearing, and then reappearing, to disappear into the wood.
> So many ways to lose sight of them, then to recapture sight of them. They are sharp at first sight . . . then smudged . . . then lost . . . then glimpsed again . . . then gone. (11)

He, too, has known the potential for contact, the potential for the bridge across the abyss but he, too, has not been and will not be able to make that contact.

One such putative contact occurs in a second pivotal point when Ellen moves toward Rumsey. They converse of things past, of things present, and of things to come. The rapidity of their shift from tense to tense, the alteration of their focus makes it impossible to discern where they are or where they ought to be. There is no enlightenment. As Ellen concludes,

> Around me sits the night. Such a silence. I can hear myself. Cup my ear. My heart beats in my ear. Such a silence. Is it me? Am I silent or speaking? How can I know? Can I know such things? No-one has ever told me. I need to be told things. I seem to be old. Am I old now? No-one will tell me. I must find a person to tell me these things. (15)

She is engaged in the process of finding a person who will tell her such things but, like the surveyor of Kafka's *The Castle* and the librarian of Borges' "The Library of Babel," the vital contact is never attained.

In the midst of such darkness, in the presence of such silence, time dissolves. In the soft sift of time's turning, little of note or of certainty remains. Ellen notes,

> After my work each day I walk back through people but I don't notice them. I'm not in a dream or anything of that sort. On the contrary. I'm quite wide awake to the world around me. But not to the people. There must be something in them to notice, to pay attention to, something of interest in them. In fact I know there is. I'm certain of it. But I pass through them noticing nothing. It is only later, in my room, that I remember. Yes, I remember. But I'm never sure that what I remember is of to-day or of yesterday or of a long time ago. (20)

In the trees dark birds or shapes like birds sit. They may be "just birds, resting after a long journey" (18) or they may be only "a shape, a shadow" (23). Thus the three characters are like the narrator of Wallace Steven's "Domination of Black," who "saw how the night came,/ Came striding like the color of the heavy hemlocks" and was afraid.

There may be a way out; there may be a way through the dark. Bates conjures with the possibility. "You cross the field out of darkness. You arrive" (21, 22). But the journey through their haunted land is forever and their return a chimera. As Ellen concludes, concludes in their behalf, "Around me sits the night. Such a silence" (25). Pinter seems to arrive, then, with Yeats in "The Stare's Nest by My Window" where

> We are closed in, and the key is turned
> On our uncertainty.

The indistinct background, the hazy setting of the London production served to reinforce the indistinct and hazy existence of the characters themselves. The individual details that surface in the dialogue might once have been rooted in the concrete, but they are cut off from their ground; they are the detritus of experiences fragmented, of visions faded, of continuity lost. The fragments of their discourse float by like debris on the tide's turn, but nowhere can one put his foot down and strike bottom. Of sounds and silence and shadow, then, are they made. Not only is Rilke's orphean question "*Wann aber sind wir?*" not answered, but one could only distrust any answer forthcoming.

As Heraclitus observed, "in the circle the beginning and the end are one." Accordingly, the inscape of *Landscape* (1968), is reminiscent of the room of Bert and Rose. But Bert and Rose are now called Duff and Beth and their room is the kitchen of a country house. But there are also important differences between *The Room* and *Landscape*. Bert and Rose could not communicate with each other because they did not understand each other's needs and because they could not speak the healing word to each other. Duff and Beth cannot talk to each other at all. In a headnote Pinter observes that Duff is apparently speaking to Beth, but he does not seem to hear her voice. Similarly, Beth does not hear Duff's voice and does not even look in his direction. The estrangement is so radical as to suggest that they are in completely different worlds even though they sit in the same room. About *The Room*, also, hovered a nameless terror, an unspoken horror that, while it might have been the projection of inner anxieties, was still "out there," still waiting to enter like Faust's poodle the moment the door opened too wide. (Sancho Panza concluded that one cannot see windmills unless one already has windmills in his head.) But the characters of *Landscape* seem trapped by another kind of perplexity. They seem isolated in time, so isolated that past and present are confused. Indeed the present is seen as a montage of the past. There will be occasions in which the past of one person will converge on the past of another, but the present is glutted with the past, too many pasts to make clarity possible any longer.

Beth opens the dialogue by saying, "I would like to stand by the sea. It is there" (7). What "it" is or where "there" is remains a mystery. Is she saying, simply, I like to stand by the beach and nothing else? Is she saying that "there" is where she really is, where she comes into the presence of herself, where *Sein* becomes *Dasein*? We are not told and Pinter does not provide sufficient evidence to make any judgment valid. There are points at which Beth and Duff seem to converge in a most indirect fashion. Completely out of any mutual context, Beth observes "I'd been in the sea" and Duff rejoins, though not by way of answering her directly, "Maybe it's something to do with the fishing. Getting to learn more about fish" (17). Such non-exchange is as close as they get to talking to each other. Only the fact that fish are known to frequent the sea makes any connection, however tenuous, possible.

From the verbal debris we do pick up a few shards, a few splinters. The couple are elderly, have worked as chauffeur and housekeeper for a man named Sykes, and sit now in an empty house, their employer dead, and their own lives unfolding an obscure logic of its own. Of the two, Duff is more stolid, more unimaginative, and seemingly more content with the fragmentation which is his life. Beth, however, seems disquieted. She lives even more in the past and often conjures memories of her lover on the beach. At one point Duff interjects, "I told you that I'd let you down. I'd been unfaithful to you" (26). But there is no response. Though Beth never acknowledges his presence, Duff continues to impose his conversation on her.

Do you like me to talk to you?
[*pause*]
Do you like me to tell you about all the things I've been doing?
[*pause*]
About all the things I've been thinking?
[*pause*]
Mmmnn?
[*pause*]
I think you do. (29, 30)

In the threnody of lives lost and past recovery, there seem moments of partial convergence. But those points of contact remain in the potential and are left unrealized. Duff, for example, thinks back on one occasion when Beth was standing by the window looking out into the darkness. What was it she was watching he wonders. Her face in the glass darkly? the darkness itself? Beth speaks then, after silence between them and not in response to his query.

I remembered always, in drawing, the basic principles of shadow and light. Objects intercepting the light cast shadows. Shadow is deprivation of light. The shape of the shadow is determined by that of the object. But not always. Not always directly. Sometimes it is only indirectly affected by it. Sometimes the cause of the shadow cannot be found. (41, 42)

The same dark birds of *Silence* preside in the trees. The domination of black affords the only light.

And so it runs. Duff and Beth gather a sum of silence about them. He remembers specific details of mundane afternoons or evenings at the pub. She continues to weave an enchanted though incomplete circle about the image of her beloved. Thus, she sits like Molly Bloom on the traverse slope of her mind, "So silent the sky in my eyes. Gently the sound of the tide. (*pause*) Oh my true love I said" (46). The play is over and the rest is silence.

Landscape and *Silence* do not, therefore, represent a fatal erring across the fragile line, a descent into something less, or more, than theatre. The intense rhythm of sound and silence, the pause and sway of language could not of itself make theatre, for theatre is still acted poetry. For all the static qualities of *Landscape* and *Silence,* however, there is movement still. Bodies are turgid and comparatively immobile, but spirits yet move through deepening shades of silence. For all their truncation, for all their visions and memories *manqué,* these characters, as Pascal reminds us in *pensée* 233, are embarked. They cannot go home again; they cannot see what they are heading toward; they are, however, irretrievably embarked. If they may not then go with the protective word, they must journey with broken words through regions of silence. For all the chaos and discordancy of their silences and ours, a poetic of the highest order emerges, a dramaturgy become thaumaturgy.

Afterword: The Poetics of Silence

When Kenneth Tynan criticized Pinter on a BBC interview for not dealing with ideas and for not revealing his characters more, Pinter replied that he was only trying to push his characters to "the extreme edge of their living, where they are living pretty much alone." Pinter's concern is not with the "struggling proletariate" of the social realists or even with an abstract notion of "man," but rather with the concrete experience of being human. His characters are found neither at the barricades nor behind the threatened panoplies of power. They are lonely, frightened individuals who have returned to the privacy of their rooms to have a think. They are kings and counselors without their regalia. They are all, under the skin, shivering creatures who fear the silences around them.

Pinter explained his point of view in another reflection.

I am interested primarily in people: I want to present living people to the audience, worthy of their interest primarily because they *are*, they exist, not because of any moral the author may draw from them.[1]

Our dramatic experience, then, must arise out of our recognition of fellow creatures and not out of our assent to what those creatures happen to believe or disbelieve. The author has lived the dream of the play countless times before he finally lends it form and substance. The audience initially enters the dream of the play in comparative innocence but soon begins to find bits and pieces of its own dream of life in that play. To find such points of contact between separate dreams is the end of all aesthetic communication. There is, finally, no hortative moral to draw from Pinter's plays, no

122

deontological road map to guide us though his work does remind us that the dream we dream is communal.

It has been the thesis of this study that Pinter's special dramatic gift is the gift of tongues, the capacity to hear and reproduce the sound of silence. Each of the plays discussed revealed a rhythmic exchange of sound and silence that communicated when communication was not supposed to be possible. In his *History of Form in German Literature,* Klopstock described how "the wordless quality moves within a good poem like the gods in Homer's battles, seen only by a few." Perhaps Pinter's greatest contribution is to rediscover the wordless quality of our language, to recover what Rilke called the "language where languages end."

Pinter's particular achievement has been to sustain linguistically the sort of tensions which seem to drive his characters from within. The fragmentary sentence, the phrase left hanging, the awkward pause, become outer manifestations of the inner anxiety, the deeper uncertainty. The discordant clash of language in, say, *The Caretaker,* is indicative of the discord that arises not only between character and character but within each of the characters. The fumbling efforts at conversation which ensue indicate the desperate need the characters have to make themselves known. Paraphrasing von Clausewitz's definition of "war," language becomes *a continuation of tension by other means.* On such occasions, Heidegger reminds us, language seems not so much a faculty that man possesses as that which possesses man.

But the "continuation of tension" may not always have the exchange of information as its goal. Many of Pinter's characters, on the contrary, go to some length to evade being known by others. The sounds these characters exchange are a holding action, a skirmish designed to avoid the larger confrontation. Pinter describes such a strategy, "communication itself between people is so frightening that rather than do that there is continual cross-talk, a continual talking about other things rather than what is at the root of their relationship." [2] One source of this circumvention of communication may derive from opposing levels of knowledge or intelligence. In *The Birthday Party,* for example, Goldberg and McCann can badger Stanley to distraction because of their continued reference to unknown forces or significant but hidden events. Or, as in *The Caretaker*, Mick can keep ahead of Davies because of his superior intelligence and wit. But the more important source of evasion arises out of the character's fear that if he reveals himself, if he comes clean, he will be at the mercy of those who know him. Davies, for example, will never admit much about Sidcup and expose his illusion. Everything he says then, however insignifiant it seems, remains a part of his larger attempt to learn vital details about others and keep his own secrets to himself.

When we examine the individual lines of dialogue which Pinter has assembled, we may see no special significance in them. They seem the language of ordinary men with ordinary preoccupations. But if we examine the same fragments within the total context of the play, we discover that they take on an added import. We begin to perceive, for example, cross-references which weave an allusive fabric, a fabric which in turn serves as a context for otherwise isolated events. Even though the "truth" of one conversation may seem to be negated or called in question by the "truth" of another conversation, we learn that there is a subtle rhythm in the stichomythia of the characters, a rhythm which is not apparent at first. Those who had the pleasure of seeing Zero Mostel and Burgess Meredith in *Waiting for Godot* were startled to discover the poise and balance of lines which appeared lifeless and unrelated on the printed page. The same phenomenon occurs when Pinter's dialogue is brought to life on the stage. The same attention to detail which seems trivial in the reading produces a rise and fall of suspense in the staging. The pauses force the audience as well as the characters to consider the possible responses available. The pauses, then, are not empty but are filled with expectations seeking to be engendered.

The subtle beauty of Pinter's quotidian language arises from its capacity to tell us more about the characters who use that language than they are capable of telling us themselves. Like all lyric poets, Pinter's first obligation is to the *how* of communication and not to the *what*. If such mundane language seems mysterious and terror-ridden, it is only because the lives of men who use a worn-out language are mysterious and terror-ridden. The realist usually sets out to employ the language of common men and succeeds in re-producing only what he thinks is the language of common men. Paradoxically, Pinter's success in attuning our ear to the everyday modes of discourse makes it possible for us to recover the strangeness, the mystery inherent in common human experience. The way of the one realist leads to a positivism of the viscera, the way of the other to a phenom-enology of the spirit.

The criticism leveled against Pinter has often been directed more at what he does not do than what he does. Much of this criticism has concomitantly lacked sensitivity to what it is that Pinter really is doing. Perhaps the most serious and systematic criticism has been raised by Amend with five particular objections.[3] First, Amend argues, Pinter introduces symbols and then does not complete them. (The Buddha of *The Caretaker* might be an example.) It is true that Pinter introduces a number of non-symbols, symbols which do not communicate. But we must understand these non-symbols to be a part of the *Weltanschauung* of the play, a *Weltan-schauung* in which the correspondences have broken down, in which the symbols, to use Tillich's designation, are bro-ken. Secondly, Amend charges Pinter with being overly am-biguous. This criticism is related to the first and behind it lingers a desire that the world be made intelligible whether it is or not. Nevertheless it is true that Pinter often willfully suppresses the motives and background of his characters. The question then remains whether the author is merely being coy or giving life to a situation out of which obscurity seems a natural consequence. Drama is the externalization of the *telos* within and one suspects that the obscurity of Pinter's plays reflects his attempt to respond with fidelity to the incognito name and nature of our universe. Pinter will resort to no *deus ex machina*, no secret will, no lost cousin to unravel the reticulated web of human experience.

Amend's third stricture may be premature. Insofar as Pinter is concerned with the problem of communication, there are only so many things one can do to communicate incommunication. Thus, Amend argues, Pinter risks repeating himself. It may be true that one cannot communicate incommunication with originality forever; but one can continue to communicate the various motives of those who do not wish, or cannot effect, communication. In either case Pinter will have to be allowed the right to develop in his own time and fashion.

The fourth charge against Pinter is probably justified. Amend concludes that not only are Pinter's characters "grubby" in person, but they are "grubby" in soul as well. So what, one wonders. Are all characters to be of aristotelian stature? Obviously not. Sophocles' characters may have manifested man's tragic stature in his war with the gods. But Pinter's characters show us our ironic stature in the war with ourselves in a time when the gods have withdrawn. Both dramatists serve their fellows well, each in his own way.

The final criticism Amend advances is that Pinter has a negative approach to values. Behind this last criticism lurks a call for the "right" values, the "right" ideas, maybe even the "right" kind of politics. But Pinter refuses to trade his aesthetic gain in the noisy barter of the market place. One may be well-advised to remember also the observation of Hermes Trismegistus that things above are copies of things below. The artist who is true to his calling may find it necessary in our time to work by way of what Hopper has called "negative disclosure."

Pinter is, as every artist should be who would be true to his vision, especially suspicious of the critics. In his essay "Writing for the Theatre," he notes that the primary difference between the week-long run of *The Birthday Party* and the extended run of *The Caretaker* was that he used dashes in the former and dots in the latter to indicate pauses or breaks in the dialogue. The fact that in neither case could one hear the dots and dashes, he observes, did not fool the critics who soon tumbled to the difference. Pinter is jesting in order to make a point although with the very serious intention of making his indifference to criticism known.[4] The more important fact is that critics were listening to those pauses. They were listening to the spaces between words which are there whether Pinter put them there or simply recorded accurately what he heard around him. Just as the artist must make a number of sensitive critical judgments so the critic must attune himself to the kind of decisions that the artist has in fact made. In that same essay Pinter goes on to describe the creative process as he experiences it.

You arrange *and* you listen, following the clues you leave for yourself, through the characters. And sometimes a balance is found, where image can freely engender image and where at the same time you are able to keep your sights on the place where the characters are silent and in hiding. It is in the silence that they are most evident to me.[5]

Critics of Pinter will necessarily have to refocus their attention on what Pinter is doing rather than what he is not doing. They must look behind his language to discover what is really being said.

A British psychoanalyst has noted that "there is a prophecy in Amos that a time will come when there will be a famine in the land, 'not a famine for bread, nor a thirst for water, but of *hearing* the words of the Lord.' That time has now come to pass. It is the present age." [6] Perhaps this is an hour of famine for hearing. The kind of hearing necessary to experience Pinter's drama fully is not a simple matter, for Pinter's language is not the rhetoric of direction but the rhetoric of association. One word can, like a pebble in a pond, send out an infinite number of circles. One word may not only lead to another but will more often stir some forgotten experience of pain or pleasure; however, that which ensues is not more language but more silence. This is the silence which speaks although it is as MacLeish describes in "Ars Poetica,"

> wordless
> As the flight of birds.

We have also seen how Pinter's communicative process involves not so much the rhetoric of direction as the rhetoric of silent gesture. In a 1968 CBS television special on "The Actor" Pinter recalled how he had once been a member of Sir Donald Wolfit's company. Then, contrasting the histrionic style of that company, symbolized by the flourishing of a cape, Pinter described his own strategy for the "taking of dramatic moments. There are moments in which the movements are very exact and seemingly very trivial—when a glass is moved from there to there." [He moved a glass about six inches.] "This is a very big moment." [Then, after a pause] "It is in the silences when they stop speaking to each other and then speak. . . ." Though his means may differ, Pinter's "taking of the dramatic moment" places him in accord with the Western dramatic tradition, with the whole idea of theatre itself.

The attempt to recover the poetics of silence is not unique to Pinter. Norman O. Brown records the early concern of Apollonius of Tyana for the *logos* of silence. To hear the *logos* of silence is to have ears to hear what is left unsaid. Apollonius asked further that we "not wonder that I know all languages since I know what men do not say." [7] More recent appraisals of silence must include Rilke who affirms,

> *Schweigen. Wer inniger schweig,*
> *rührt an die Wurzeln der Rede.*
>
> (Silence. Who fervently remains silent
> touches the roots of speech.)

One also thinks of the movement initiated in the 1920's by Jean-Jacques Bernard who called for "a theatre of silence" to articulate those emotions which could not be raised to language. In *The Theatre and Its Double*, Artaud argued for the silent language of gesture thinking that there "is a poetry of the senses as there is a poetry of language, and that this concrete physical language to which I refer is truly theatrical only to the degree that the thoughts it expresses are beyond the reach of the spoken language." But Pinter operates without a conscious dramaturgy of silence. His tradition is not so much that of Stanislavski with his "sub-texts" as the ancient silences of the Kabuki and the mime. The silences of his plays are not programmatic; they are dramatic. The difference is between theory and practice; the difference is between a philosophy of experience and a technique forged from the dross of experience.

Sartre and others argue that the artist today must be "engaged"; thus one form of commitment or another is often demanded of our artists. But even the social violence of our time must finally be extirpated from the psyche of individual men. The nature of Pinter's "commitment," if one must use that word, is to the quest within and not the program without. Yeats wisely wondered why we give medals to soldiers when the artist wages a far more courageous, far more lonely battle within himself. Pinter's particular kind of courage is to try to say what seems to lie beyond the saying.

The creative act has never been easy and perhaps it is even more difficult in an age when our language as our souls suffers the sickness unto death. Pinter acutely describes how the sickness unto death is the lot of even the artist whose gift is language.

I have another strong feeling about words which amounts to nothing less than nausea. Such a weight of words confronts us day in, day out, words spoken in a context such as this, words written by me and by others, the bulk of it a stale dead terminology; ideas endlessly repeated and permutated become platitudinous, trite, meaningless. Given this nausea, it's very easy to be overcome by it and step back into paralysis. I imagine most writers know something of this kind of paralysis. But if it is possible to confront this nausea, to follow it to its hilt, to move through it and out of it, then it is possible to say that something has occurred, that something has even been achieved.[8]

To confront this nausea is the crucial problem of the age. The artist cannot heal our shattered bones or mend the rent fabric of our society, but he may make it possible for us to remain human amid the silence of our infinite spaces. Only then can life approximate what Pinter has called writing, "a kind of celebration."[9]

Notes

Prologue

1. Harold Pinter, "Writing for the Theatre," *The New British Drama*, ed. Henry Popkin (New York, 1964), p. 576.
2. George Steiner, *Language and Silence: Essays on Language, Literature and the Inhuman* (New York, 1967), p. ix.
3. As Hopper has noted, "The quest is not outward, but inward. It is a descent into the void of contemporary lostness: a descent in which the moment in time is our only possession, but a time in which there is no fullness."—Stanley Romaine Hopper, "The Problem of Moral Isolation in Contemporary Literature," *Spiritual Problems in Contemporary Literature*, ed. S. R. Hopper (New York, 1957), p. 154.
4. Frederick Hoffman, *Samuel Beckett: The Language of Self* (New York, 1964), p. 59.
5. Jacques Guicharnaud, *Modern French Theatre from Giraudoux to Beckett* (New Haven, 1961), p. 232.
6. The epithet "comedies of menace" has often been used by critics of Pinter.
7. Stanley Romaine Hopper, "Irony—The Pathos of the Middle," *Crosscurrents* (Winter 1962), pp. 31 ff.
8. Harold Pinter, "Pinterview," *Newsweek*, LX (July 23, 1962), 69.
9. Unpubl. diss. (University of Wisconsin, 1965) by Jack Frisch, "Ironic Theatre: Techniques of Irony in the Plays of Samuel Beckett, Eugene Ionesco, Harold Pinter and Jean Genet," p. 137.
10. Ruby Cohn, "The World of Harold Pinter," *Tulane Drama Review*, VI (March 1962), 56.
11. Tom Stoppard, *Rosencrantz and Guildenstern Are Dead* (New York, 1967), p. 39.

12. George E. Wellwarth, *The Theatre of Protest and Paradox* (New York, 1967), p. 197.

13. Harold Pinter, "The Art of the Theatre III," *The Paris Review*, 39 (Fall 1966), 19.

14. Alan Sillitoe, "Novel or Play?" *Twentieth Century*, 169 (February 1961), 209.

15. Harold Pinter, interview with Kenneth Tynan, BBC Home Service, 28 October 1960.

16. Harold Pinter, "The Art of the Theatre III," p. 17.

17. *Ibid.*, p. 27.

18. Eric Bentley, *The Playwright as Thinker* (New York, 1960), p. 241.

19. R. D. Laing, *The Politics of Experience* (New York, 1967), p. 22.

20. Harold Pinter, "Writing for the Theatre," p. 579.

21. Carl G. Jung, *Symbols of Transformation* (London, 1956), p. 15.

The Room as Metaphor

1. Certainly the withdrawal from a hostile environment into a protective redoubt is a recurrent psychological theme in contemporary literature. Hemingway's "A Clean Well-lighted Place" is a ready example.

2. Susan Sontag, *Against Interpretation* (New York, 1966), p. 8.

3. Harold Pinter, "Writing for Myself," *Twentieth Century*, 169 (February 1961), 173.

4. Charles Marowitz, " 'Pinterism' Is Maximum Tension Through Minimum Information," *New York Times Magazine*, October 1, 1967, p. 92.

5. The act of "naming" is central to *The Room*. Mrs. Sands confuses Mr. Hudd with Mr. Kidd; the Sands' argue over "sitting" and "perching"; Rose tells Riley that his real name is something else; and Riley calls Rose "Sal." To have a name is to have an identity and the separate instances in which the names are in doubt contribute to the largest pattren of *The Room* in which a lonely woman finds her identity in question.

6. Harold Pinter, "The Art of the Theatre III," *The Paris Review*, 39 (Fall 1966), 31.

7. F. J. Bernhard, "Beyond Realism: The Plays of Harold Pinter," *Modern Drama*, III (September 1965), 191.

8. Harold Pinter, "Writing for the Theatre," *The New British Drama*, ed. Henry Popkin (New York, 1964), p. 574.

9. For example, Stanley seems to know the Irish air that McCann whistles (50).

10. Jacqueline Hoefer, "Pinter and Whiting: Two Attitudes Towards the Alienated Artist," *Modern Drama*, IV (February 1962), 402.

11. This point of view is suggested by Bernard Dukore, "The Theatre of Harold Pinter," *Tulane Drama Review*, VI (March 1962), 52.

12. George E. Wellwarth, *The Theatre of Protest and Paradox* (New York, 1967), p. 204.

13. Cited by Martin Esslin, *The Theatre of the Absurd* (Garden City, 1961), p. 205.

14. James Boulton, "Harold Pinter: *The Caretaker* and Other Plays," *Modern Drama*, VI (September 1963), 135.

15. Pinter, "Writing for the Theatre," p. 575.

The Poverty of Self

1. There are other echoes of the Barnabas of *The Castle* in *A Slight Ache*. Consider, for example, "K. had been studying his face the whole time, and now he gave it a last survey. Barnabas was about the same height as K., but his eyes seemed to look down on K., yet that was almost in a kind of humility; it was impossible to think that this man could put anyone to shame."

2. The television plays *The Tea Party* and *The Basement* were unsuccessfully revived off-Broadway in October of 1968. Perhaps Walter Kerr's review in the *Times* of 3 November 1968 was typical of the critical response afforded the opening. "It is as though Pinter had snapped on his electric typewriter and let the machine do the play out of memory. Even the memory has evocative echoes, but the visit to familiar haunts is this time tired and tiring."

3. Eugene Ionesco, *Notes and Counter Notes* (New York, 1964), p. 180.

4. George E. Wellwarth, *The Theatre of Protest and Paradox* (New York, 1967), p. 211.

5. Harold Pinter, "Writing for the Theatre," *The New British Drama*, ed. Henry Popkin (New York, 1964), p. 579.

The Struggle for Possession

1. To open the Pinter puzzle box a bit further, one might also expect that there will be a collection of interpretations as well.

2. One may also observe the acceptance of multiple truths,

multiple realities in Pirandello's *Right You Are, If You Think You Are* or in Borges' "The Garden of Forking Paths."

3. John Russell Taylor, *Anger and After* (Harmondsworth, Middlesex, 1963), p. 310.

4. Arnold P. Hinchliffe, *Harold Pinter* (New York, 1967), p. 117.

5. This point of view is also argued by James Boulton, "Harold Pinter: *The Caretaker* and Other Plays," *Modern Drama*, VI (September 1963), 131 ff.

6. Richard Schechner, "Puzzling Pinter," *Tulane Drama Review*, XI (Winter 1966), 176.

7. Harold Pinter, "The Art of the Theatre III," *The Paris Review*, 39 (Fall 1966), 34.

8. Martin Esslin, *The Theatre of the Absurd* (Garden City, 1961), p. 211.

9. Pinter, "The Art of the Theatre III," p. 30. Pinter resists localizing the outside threat in any institutional form. Only once has he written a specifically satiric play, *The Hothouse*, a full-length drama written after *The Caretaker*. *The Hothouse* was written from the side of the hierarchy who run an asylum filled with nameless patients. But, because he thought the characters wooden and the tone didactic, Pinter discarded the manuscript.

10. Robert Brustein, *Seasons of Discontent: Dramatic Opinions 1959–65* (New York, 1965), p. 181.

11. Pinter has admitted, "I feel a sense of music continually in writing, which is a different matter from having been influenced by it."—"Art of the Theatre III," p. 20.

12. Harold Pinter, "On Filming 'The Caretaker,'" *Transatlantic Review*, 13 (Summer 1963), 24.

13. *Ibid.*, p. 19.

14. Bernard Dukore, "The Theatre of Harold Pinter," *Tulane Drama Review*, VI (March 1962), 50.

15. Harold Pinter, "Harold Pinter Replies," *New Theatre Magazine*, XI (January 1961), 9.

16. *Ibid.*, p. 10.

17. Victor Amend, "Harold Pinter—Some Credits and Debits," *Modern Drama*, X (September 1967), 166.

18. Pinter, "The Art of the Theatre III," p. 17.

19. Hinchliffe, *Harold Pinter* (New York, 1967), Preface.

The Homecoming

1. Pinter's shorter plays often make for more effective theatre

because they are more intense and concentrated. *The Homecoming* takes a situation partially adumbrated in *A Slight Ache* and elsewhere and expands it to full-length. Thus *The Homecoming* runs the risk of saying what has already been said and seeming either one act too long or one situation too short.

2. David Benedictus, *The Spectator* (June 11, 1965), cited in Arnold Hinchliffe, *Harold Pinter* (New York, 1967), p. 151.

3. Robert Kemper, "One Man's Family," *Christian Century*, 84 (March 1, 1967), 276 f.

4. A. N. Franzblau, "A Psychiatrist Looks at *The Homecoming*," *Saturday Review* (April 8, 1967), p. 58 *passim*.

5. Kelly Morris, "*The Homecoming*," *Tulane Drama Review*, XI (Winter 1966), 186.

6. At least one production (Purdue University, Summer 1968) utilized an amplified heart beat at crucial points to dramatize the tension. The resemblance to a primitive tom-tom was hard to ignore.

7. Morris, pp. 186 f.

8. John Warner, "Can You Go Home Again: The Epistemological Quest in Pinter's *The Homecoming*," *Contemporary Literature*, forthcoming, 1970.

9. Cited by Hinchliffe, p. 178.

10. This interpretation borders dangerously and may even blunder into the kind of allegory that has been resisted previously in this book. Certainly Pinter would deny any such interpretation as nonsense; nevertheless, I persist in believing that the deepest movement of the play is in the direction of unification with the "Other," the archetypal experience of homecoming.

11. Henry Hewes, "Probing Pinter's Plays," *Saturday Review* (April 8, 1967), p. 56.

12. Stanley Romaine Hopper, "The Problem of Moral Isolation in Contemporary Literature," *Spiritual Problems in Contemporary Literature*, ed. S. R. Hopper (New York, 1957), p. 161.

The Rest Is Silence

1. Or as Francis Fergusson notes in his edition of *The Poetics*, "*action*, (*praxis*) does not mean deeds, events, or physical activity: it means, rather, the motivation from which deeds spring." Aristotle, *The Poetics*, ed. Francis Fergusson (New York, 1963), p. 8.

Afterword: The Poetics of Silence

1. Cited by John Russell Taylor, *Anger and After* (Harmondsworth, Middlesex, 1963), p. 296.

2. *Ibid.*

3. Victor Amend, "Harold Pinter—Some Credits and Debits," *Modern Drama*, X (September 1967), 173 f.

4. It is a good thing for even the critics that Pinter is not easily intimidated. The first Düsseldorf performance of *The Caretaker* was raucously booed. In the European tradition the author took a bow with the cast—or rather they took thirty-four bows until only two of the disgruntled patrons were left.

5. Harold Pinter, "Writing for the Theatre," *The New British Drama*, ed. Henry Popkin (New York, 1964), p. 579.

6. R. D. Laing, *The Politics of Experience* (New York, 1967), p. 101.

7. Norman O. Brown, *Love's Body* (New York, 1966), p. 256.

8. Pinter, "Writing for the Theatre," p. 578.

9. *Ibid.*, p. 580.

Selected Bibliography

Primary Materials

"The Art of the Theatre III," *The Paris Review*, No. 39 (Fall 1966), 13–37.

The Birthday Party, and The Room. New York, 1961.

The Caretaker, and The Dumb Waiter. New York, 1965.

"Dialogue for Three," *Strand*, VI (1963–64), 4–5.

"The Examination," *The Collection and The Lover.* London, 1964.

"Harold Pinter Replies," *New Theatre Magazine*, XI (January 1961), 8–10.

The Homecoming. New York, 1966.

Landscape. London, 1968.

The Lover, Tea Party, The Basement. New York, 1967.

Mac. London, 1968.

A Night Out, Night School, Revue Sketches. New York, 1968.

Pinter, Harold, and Clive Donner. "On Filming 'The Caretaker,'" *Transatlantic Review*, 13 (Summer 1963), 17–26.

Silence. London, 1968.

Three Plays: A Slight Ache, The Collection, The Dwarfs. New York, 1962.

"Writing for Myself," *Twentieth Century*, 169 (February 1961), 172–75.

"Writing for the Theatre," *The New British Drama*, ed. Henry Popkin. New York, 1964.

Secondary Materials

BOOKS

Abel, Lionel. *Metatheatre: A New View of Dramatic Form.* New York, 1963.

Aristotle. *The Poetics*, ed. Francis Fergusson. New York, 1963.

Artaud, Antonin. *The Theatre and its Double*. New York, 1958.

Bentley, Eric. *The Playwright As Thinker*. New York, 1960.

Brown, Norman O. *Love's Body*. New York, 1966.

Brustein, Robert. *Seasons of Discontent: Dramatic Opinions 1959–1965*. New York, 1965.

Esslin, Martin. *The Theatre of the Absurd*. Garden City, 1961.

Evans, Ifor. *A Short History of English Drama*. Boston, 1965.

Fergusson, Francis. *The Idea of a Theater*. Garden City, 1953.

Fowlie, Wallace. *A Guide to Contemporary French Literature*. New York, 1962.

Freedman, Morris. *The Moral Impulse: Modern Drama from Ibsen to the Present*. Carbondale, Ill., 1967.

Frisch, Jack. *Ironic Theatre: Techniques of Irony in the Plays of Samuel Beckett, Eugene Ionesco, Harold Pinter and Jean Genet*. Unpubl. diss. University of Wisconsin, 1965.

Gordon, Lois G. *Stratagems to Uncover Nakedness: The Dramas of Harold Pinter*. Columbia, Mo., 1969.

Guicharnaud, Jacques. *Modern French Theatre from Giraudoux to Beckett*. New Haven, 1961.

Hassan, Ihab. *The Literature of Silence: Henry Miller and Samuel Beckett*. New York, 1967.

Heidegger, Martin. "Remembrance of the Poet," *Existence and Being*, trans. Douglas Scott. Chicago, 1964.

Hinchliffe, Arnold P. *Harold Pinter*. New York, 1967.

Hoffman, Frederick. *Samuel Beckett: The Language of Self*. New York, 1964.

Hopper, Stanley Romaine. *Spiritual Problems in Contemporary Literature*. New York, 1957.

Ionesco, Eugene. *Notes and Counter Notes*. New York, 1964.

Jung, Carl G. *Symbols of Transformation*. London, 1956.

Kerr, Walter. *Harold Pinter*. New York, 1967.

Kitchin, Laurence. *Mid-Century Drama*. London, 1962.

Laing, R. D. *The Politics of Experience*. New York, 1967.

Lewis, Allan. *The Contemporary Theatre*. New York, 1962.

Sontag, Susan. *Against Interpretation*. New York, 1966.

Steiner, George. *Language and Silence: Essays on Language, Literature and the Inhuman*. New York, 1967.

Styan, J. L. *The Dark Comedy*. Cambridge, 1962.

Taylor, John Russell. *Anger and After*. Harmondsworth, Middlesex, 1963.

Warshow, Robert. *The Immediate Experience*. Garden City, 1954.

Wellwarth, George E. *The Theatre of Protest and Paradox.* New York, 1967.

Wheelwright, Phillip. *The Burning Fountain.* Bloomington, Ind., 1954.

ARTICLES

Amend, Victor. "Harold Pinter—Some Credits and Debits," *Modern Drama*, X (September 1967), 165–74.

Barnes, Clive. "Harold Pinter's Debt to James Joyce," The *New York Times* (July 25, 1969), D8.

Bernhard, F. J. "Beyond Realism: The Plays of Harold Pinter," *Modern Drama*, III, 2 (September 1965), 185–91.

Bosworth, Patricia, "Why Doesn't He Write More?" The *New York Times* (October 27, 1968), D3.

Boulton, James. "Harold Pinter: *The Caretaker* and Other Plays," *Modern Drama*, VI (September 1963), 131–40.

Brown, John Russell. "Dialogue in Pinter and Others," *Critical Quarterly*, VII, 3 (Autumn 1964), 225–43.

———. "Mr. Pinter's Shakespeare," *Essays in the Modern Drama*, ed. Morris Freedman. Boston, 1964.

Callen, A. "Comedy and Passion in the Plays of Harold Pinter," *Forum for Modern Language Studies*, III, 3, 299–305.

Cohn, Ruby. "Latter Day Pinter," *Drama Survey*, III (February 1964), 367–77.

———. "The World of Harold Pinter," *Tulane Drama Review*, VI (March 1962), 55–68.

Crist, Judith. "A Mystery: Pinter on Pinter," *Look* (December 24, 1968), pp. 77–80.

Dukore, Bernard. "The Theatre of Harold Pinter," *Tulane Drama Review*, VI (March 1962), 43–54.

———. "A Woman's Place," *Quarterly Journal of Speech*, LII (October 1966), 237–41.

Esslin, Martin. "Pinter Translated," *Encounter*, 30 (March, 1968), 45–47.

Farrington, Conor. "The Language of Drama," *Tulane Drama Review*, V (December 1960), 65–72.

Franzblau, A. N. "A Psychiatrist Looks at *The Homecoming*," *Saturday Review* (April 8, 1967), 58.

Gallagher, Kent. "Harold Pinter's Dramaturgy," *Quarterly Journal of Speech*, LII (October 1966), 242–48.

Halton, Kathleen. "Pinter: Funny and Moving and Frightening," *Vogue*, 150 (October 1967), 194 *passim*.

Hewes, Henry. "Probing Pinter's Plays," *Saturday Review* (April 8, 1967), pp. 56 ff.

Hoefer, Jacqueline. "Pinter and Whiting: Two Attitudes Towards the Alienated Artist," *Modern Drama*, IV (February 1962), 402–8.

Hopper, Stanley Romaine. "Irony—The Pathos of the Middle," *Crosscurrents* (Winter 1962), 31–40.

Kemper, Robert. "One Man's Family," *Christian Century*, 84 (March 1, 1967), 276–77.

Kerr, Walter. "The Something that Pinter Holds Back," The *New York Times* (November 3, 1968), D7.

Marcus, Frank. "Pinter: The Pauses that Refresh," The *New York Times* (July 13, 1969), 8D.

Marowitz, Charles. " 'Pinterism' Is Maximum Tension Through Minimum Information," *New York Times Magazine* (October 1, 1967), pp. 36 ff.

Mast, Gerald. "Pinter's *Homecoming*," *Drama Survey*, VI (Spring 1968), 266–77.

Morris, Kelly. "*The Homecoming*," *Tulane Drama Review*, XI (Winter 1966), 185–91.

Nelson, Hugh. "The Homecoming: Kith and Kin," *Modern British Dramatists: A Collection of Essays*, ed. J. R. Brown. Englewood Cliffs, N. J., 1968, 145–63.

Pesta, John. "Pinter's Usurpers," *Drama Survey*, VI (Spring-Summer 1967), 54–65.

Schechner, Richard. "Puzzling Pinter," *Tulane Drama Review*, XI (Winter 1966), 176–84.

Sillitoe, Alan. "Novel or Play?" *Twentieth Century*, 169 (February 1961), 206–11.

Starkmann, Alfred. "*Schweigen—wörtlich genommen*," *Die Welt* (16 Juli, 1969), p. 7.

Taylor, John Russell. "British Drama of the Fifties," *On Contemporary Literature*, ed. Richard Kostelanetz. New York, 1964, pp. 90–96.

Walker, Augusta. "Messages from Pinter," *Modern Drama*, X (May 1967), 1–10.

Index

Adamov, Arthur, 4
Aesthetic communication, 122
"Angry young men," 4, 10–12
Apollinaire, Guillaume: quoted, 6
Apollonius of Tyana: quoted, 128
Archetype, 108–11
Arden, John, 11
Aristotle, 113
Arnold, Matthew: quoted, 2, 11
Artaud, Antonin, 128

Baron, David, stage name of Harold Pinter, 12
Baudelaire, Charles, 20, 47
Beckett, Samuel, 6, 8, 9, 13, 17, 53, 57, 112
Behan, Brendan, 11
Bentley, Eric: quoted, 13–14
Bernard, Jean-Jacques, 128
Blake, William: quoted, 7, 29
Borges, Jorge Luis, 9, 117, 133n2
Brecht, Bertolt, 94
Brown, Norman O., quoted, 128
Burke, Kenneth, 30

Camus, Albert, 2
Carlyle, Thomas: quoted, 15–16, 62
Clausewitz, Karl von, 123

"Comedies of Menace," 130n6
Comedy, 5–7, 47
Comedy of manners, 107
Copeau, Jacques: quoted, 52

Delaney, Shelagh, 11
Dostoevski, Fyodor, 5, 9

Eliot, T. S.: quoted, 116; mentioned, 10
Esslin, Martin, 4, 90

Fergusson, Francis: quoted, 134n1
Flaubert, Gustave: quoted, 14
Freud, Sigmund, 35
Fry, Christopher: quoted, 5–6; mentioned, 10

Genet, Jean, 9, 52, 67
Greene, Graham: quoted, 4

Hardy, Oliver, 47
Heidegger, Martin: quoted, 8–9, 96, 109, 123
Hemingway, Ernest, 9, 131n1
Heraclitus: quoted, 118
Hitchcock, Alfred, 44
Hölderlin, Friedrich: quoted, 110
Hopkins, G. M.: quoted, 3
Hopper, Stanley Romaine: quoted, 111, 126, 130n3